the Gospel *for*
MUSLIMS

the Gospel *for* MUSLIMS

An Encouragement to Share Christ
✦ ✦ ✦ with Confidence ✦ ✦ ✦

THABITI ANYABWILE

For current Information on the persecuted Church,
Please Contact:

The Voice of the Martyrs, Inc.

PO Box 443
Bartlesville, OK. 74005
(918)337-8015

MOODY PUBLISHERS

CHICAGO

Editor: Jim Vincent
Interior Design: Ragont Design
Cover Design: Faceout Studio—formerly The DesignWorks Group, Inc.
Cover Images: iStock and Getty Images

Library of Congress Cataloging-in-Publication Data

Anyabwile, Thabiti M., 1970-
The Gospel for Muslims : simple ways to share Christ with confidence / by Thabiti Anyabwile.
    p. cm.
Includes bibliographical references.
ISBN 978-0-8024-7111-6
1. Missions to Muslims. I. Title.
BV2625.A68 2010
248'.5–dc22

2009046510

We hope you enjoy this book from Moody Publishers. Our goal is to provide high-quality, thought-provoking books and products that connect truth to your real needs and challenges. For more information on other books and products written and produced from a biblical perspective, go to www.moodypublishers.com or write to:

Moody Publishers
820 N. LaSalle Boulevard
Chicago, IL 60610

1 3 5 7 9 10 8 6 4 2

Printed in the United States of America

To a faithful street preacher whose name I do not know,
who heard all of my anti-Christian arguments
and responded with gospel clarity and love.

To Derrick Scott and Sean Ensley, who prayed with concern
that I might not be eternally lost through sin and unbelief
and that the Lord would rescue me from Islam.

To a young man in my freshman dorm, Dwight,
who endured with patience my opposition and
lived joyfully and faithfully for the Lord
amid a building full of freshman pagans!

To Mack, Brian, David, Joanna, Nissen, and the
students of FOCUS
for serving the Lord in the gospel among the
Muslim people they love.

And to the Lord of Glory, who used all these
human vessels to tell me the good news of His love,
of His wrath and judgment against sin,
of His atoning sacrifice on behalf of sinners,
of His resurrection and reign, of His second coming,
of eternal life through repentance and faith in Him,
and of the blessed hope and joy of beholding His face.

Contents

Foreword   9

Why This Book?   13

Introduction: The Triumph of the Gospel in a Muslim's Life   17

Part 1: The Gospel

   1. God by Any Other Name?   27

   2. Man's Sin: Resting Lightly on the Muslim Conscience   41

   3. Jesus Christ: Fully God and Fully Man   55

   4. Jesus Christ: The Lamb Slain—and Resurrected!   67

   5. Response: There's Repentance and Faith . . .
      and Then There Is Repentance and Faith!   79

Part 2: As You Witness

   6. Be Filled with the Spirit   95

   7. Trust the Bible   107

   8. Be Hospitable   119

   9. Use Your Local Church   135

  10. Suffer for the Name   149

  11. The Good News for African-American Muslims   163

Afterword   171

Notes   173

Foreword

"Don't ya' think when we pray to God . . . and they pray to Allah . . ."

We were at a missions conference focused on world evangelization. The questioner was involved with Christian media, but his patronizing look assumed any reasonable person would of course agree with the generous assessment he was about to make.

". . . Don't ya' think that we're talking to the same God?" he concluded.

"Well, no," I said. "Actually, I think that's really a dangerous way to think."

"Dangerous?" He stared at me. "Why's that?"

"Well," I said, "sure, there are some similarities between the two faiths, especially if we're talking about certain moral actions. But when we talk about the most important things —things like how to know God—to confuse the God of Islam with the God of the Bible confuses the gospel, the very point of our eternal salvation."

I wish I could have given him the book you hold in your hands. There's no confusion with Thabiti. In fact, this is a book I've been wanting for a long time, for four important reasons.

Thabiti is compassionate. Though I have never seen him shirk from the truth, I have never seen him be unkind either. His manner is filled with grace and truth, and that comes out in this book.

Thabiti is bold. I've watched him speak of Jesus in a large gathering of Muslim people, the vast majority who were friendly, a couple who were very angry, and all who disagreed. Yet he worked to honor God, not man, by speaking the complete truth of the cross. After all, Thabiti understands what's at stake. He crossed the line himself from Islam to Christianity. I have seen Thabiti put his faith on the line with Muslim friends time and again.

Third, in a world awash with methods and techniques, Thabiti spells out clearly that the most important method to be equipped for sharing our faith with our Muslim friends and neighbors is to know the gospel through and through. He calls us to trust that the gospel is truly "the power of God unto salvation." If you know the gospel, you have the most important tool there is to share your faith with a Muslim friend.

Finally, Thabiti calls on all Christians to sharpen their faith. Orthodox Islamic doctrine is eerily similar to counterfeit Christianity: Muslims believe that Jesus was merely a prophet, not God; they believe our good works gain us entrance to heaven. They believe that the Bible is corrupted and though it contains some words from God, it's not *the*

Word of God. They believe substitutionary atonement is a scandal and that God would never allow His Son to suffer the horror of a blood sacrifice on the cross. Besides, they say, we're not that sinful anyway.

Don't these orthodox doctrines of Islam sound like nominal and popular misconceptions of Christianity in the West? For years I've heard that God helps those who help themselves; that Jesus was just a great moral teacher; that the Bible is full of errors. Today, even penal substitutionary atonement on the cross is under attack and painted as cosmic child abuse. Is it any wonder my media friend at the missions conference is confused about to whom we're praying? Thabiti calls us to sharpen our thinking about the basic foundations of the Christian faith so we know what it is we're to be talking about.

J. Mack Stiles
Chief Executive Officer, Gulf Digital Solutions
General Secretary of Fellowship of Christian
Students, United Arab Emirates

Why This Book?

Jonathan asked me an all-too-frequent question following a workshop on Muslim evangelism: "How do you share the gospel with Muslims? I feel so unequipped."

It's a fine question, but it has a fatal flaw. It assumes that somehow Muslims require a different gospel or a special technique, that Muslims are somehow impervious to the gospel in a way that other sinners are not.

This little book is written to the Jonathans who ask that question or have that feeling of being ill-equipped. It's written for the average Christian to make one basic point: As a Christian you already know everything you need to know to effectively share the good news of Jesus Christ with Muslim people. The same message that saves us—the gospel—is the message that will eternally change our Muslim neighbors and friends.

In my experience, Christians know the gospel. They simply lack confidence in its power. This book is a call to place our confidence in the message that contains God's power to save all who believe (Romans 1:16). We don't need new techniques for sharing the faith. We need confidence in the gospel when it comes to Muslim evangelism. It's my fervent prayer that this little volume encourages "Joe Christian" in what he already knows to be true so that he will share it joyfully and boldly with others.

The Gospel for Muslims is not a book on apologetics—how to defend the Christian faith. Apologetics is a helpful discipline, but it is not evangelism. The Gospel for Muslims is concerned not with defense but with a good offense, with getting the gospel out to others. So what you'll find here are helps in starting conversations, avoiding some mistakes, an indication of my failures in evangelism, and biblical lessons aimed at helping us tell the story of God's love and redemption through His Son, Jesus.

The book is organized in two sections. Part 1 focuses on the gospel itself. We cover key gospel topics—God, man, Jesus, repentance, and faith—so that the basics are explored. We touch on both Muslim and Christian understandings of these teachings so the differences are highlighted and our evangelism can be focused in helpful ways. We make references to the Quran so the reader has at least a simple introduction to some of its teachings. When we mention suras in the Quran, that's equivalent to a chapter. Ayats are verses. But we focus primarily on the Bible itself. So reading this book with Bible in hand will help the reader focus on key beliefs.

Part 2 offers some practical suggestions when approaching evangelistic discussions with Muslims. Among the suggestions and helps are chapters on the Bible, hospitality, the local church, and suffering in evangelism.

Increasingly, God seems pleased to bring the Muslim world right to our doorsteps. The work of cross-cultural evangelism and missions has never been more accessible. With some confidence and reliance on God and His gospel, we may yet be the generation that sees history's greatest revival among Muslim peoples.

That's my prayer. And I pray this book encourages every reader to be a part of God's great work.

Introduction:

The Triumph of the Gospel
In a Muslim's Life

She was a very attractive professional woman in her midtwenties. It was clear she attended the discussion of Islam at the invitation of a friend. She stood patiently, locking onto every word, as others in turn asked their questions and filed away. Finally, the crowd dwindled, and she shyly and politely thanked me for the talk.

Then the look. I've seen the look a number of times before. In an instant, a once forbidden but now ineffable joy broke across her face. Tears streamed down but her face beamed brightly. Her eyes grew slightly wild with excitement. She told me that her family was from Iran. She now lived and worked in the United States with her parents. And as is custom, she will live under their care in their home until she marries. But she has a secret. In the last two weeks she has heard the gospel of Jesus Christ and she now loves Him as her Savior.

"I don't know how to tell my parents, or what will happen. But I have never been happier in my life. I can't explain it. . . . I'm just so joyful." More tears. More beaming brightness.

The gospel "is the power of God for salvation to everyone who believes, to the Jew first and also to the Greek" (Romans 1:16 NASB)—and also to the Muslim!

I sometimes think Christians doubt this wonderful truth—that the gospel is the triumphing power of God in the lives of anyone and everyone who believes. We sometimes seem to think that certain people are beyond the saving reach of the gospel. Too often we certainly seem to think that the Muslim is beyond gospel reach and impervious to gospel power.

But contrary to our unbelief, the gospel of Jesus Christ is indeed triumphing in the hearts, minds, and lives of countless men and women from various Muslim backgrounds. I am one such person.

I've spent a significant portion of my life lost. Being separated from God by my sin, I've been dedicated to many activities, thoughts, and attitudes contrary to the gospel. But this was never truer than when I lived as a practicing Muslim.

I converted to Islam while a sophomore in college. In the years leading up to my conversion, I had grown very angry with life. My father left when I was about fourteen years old. I was angry with him. Just before my junior year in high school, I was arrested, and many of my friends distanced themselves from me. I was angry at them as well. Between my senior year in high school and freshman year of college, I discovered 1960s radicals like Malcolm X, Amiri, Baraka, and a host of others. They made me angrier. As I read the history of Africans and African Americans, I grew angry toward white people in general. By the time I completed my freshman year of college, I was a young, hotheaded militant seething with not just anger but hatred.

It was Islam that promised a way of handling and using that hatred. That's what it promised. But in my experience, what it delivered was far different.

My anger and hatred toward whites found an easy and ultimate representative target in a blond-haired, blue-eyed Jesus. Though I expressed respect for "the real Jesus," who was a prophet of Allah, I was an enemy of the cross. It was my delight to oppose Christian students on campus and to launch any argument I could against Christianity. I denied the resurrection and harangued as simple-minded fools those who believed it. Christianity was a great plot by the misguided and deceitful "followers" of the "real Jesus." I was zealous for Islam, "the perfect religion for the African American."

It was Ramadan, a time of great spiritual discipline, prayer, and study. I rose before sunrise to read the Quran and prepare for morning prayer. The morning still wore the drowsiness of sleep. I settled into my desk chair. And as I read the Quran, a steady awareness settled over me: *Islam cannot be true.*

As a Muslim, I had devoured as much of the Quran as I could. Passages that would help me speak to Christians about their "errors and misguided opinions" were of particular interest. That meant I had to consider the Quran's teachings about Jesus. But what I found simply could not be true and Islam itself be consistent.

The Quran plainly taught that Jesus was born of a virgin with no earthly father (Sura 3:42–50). The Quran plainly taught that the Torah, Psalms of David, and the Gospels were books revealed by Allah (Sura 4:163–65; 5:46–48; and 6:91–92). And in many passages, the Quran—written approximately six hundred years after Christ and the apostles—expressed such confidence in these sections of the Bible that it called people to judge the truth using the Bible (Sura 3:93–94; 5:47; and 10:94). And nowhere does the Quran teach that the Bible was corrupted or changed, only that some have covered its meaning, misunderstood it, or forgotten the message. So, for me, any consistent and intellectually honest Muslim had to come to grips with the teaching of the Bible.

And when I went to the Bible—first assuming I'd find things confirming or pointing to the Quran, and then growing desperate to find the supposed prophecies that point to Muhammad—all my assumptions were confounded and without basis. Islam was not true. Islam's claim to be the final and seal of all religions, its prophet the final and seal of all prophets, simply did not hold water.

How could Jesus be virgin born, as the Quran taught, and not be the Son of God as the Gospels so clearly teach? How could the theme of atonement and sacrifice so pronounced in both the law of Moses and the Gospels simply vanish in Islam? And most troubling of all, how could my unrighteousness and sin ever be atoned for without a perfect sacrifice on my behalf?

My sin was real and Islam offered no real solution for it.

Islam had strong-armed me into believing that all of life's needs and questions were answered by its system of laws and rituals. I had believed Islam's account of the development of religion and society—"Judaism is the elementary school, Christianity the high school, but Islam the university." A false theology and ideology had dominated my life.

By the time I emerged from this period of study and exploration, I was convinced Islam was not true. More than that, I was fairly certain that all religions were false. Rather than turn to Christ, I turned to the pursuit of the world and decided to trust myself rather than God.

In the midst of this idolatrous pursuit, the Lord intercepted and humbled me when my wife miscarried our first child. I sat in a mild depression watching television. For reasons I could not then explain, I sat transfixed as a television preacher expounded 2 Timothy 2:15. It wasn't a particularly evangelistic message, but life and power filled this sermon on studying God's Word and Christian habits of the mind.

Eventually, my wife and I visited the church where this pastor served. We were seven or eight rows from the pulpit. Crowded into a church service of some seven or eight thousand, it seemed the only people in the room were the preacher and myself.

The sermon, taken from Exodus 32, was titled "What does it take to make you angry?" Imagine that. Having been consumed with anger for well over a decade by then, the first time I entered a church since becoming a Muslim, the preacher addresses anger. But it was not what I thought. The sermon carefully examined sin, idolatry, and their consequences. The pastor challenged the congregation to develop a righteous, godly indignation toward sin, to hate sin, and to turn to God.

I sat gripped as the holiness and justice of God were unfolded from the Scripture. I grew strangely remorseful and alert, awakened really, as the pastor applied the doctrine of sin to his hearers. I was convicted, guilty before this holy God who judges all unrighteousness.

Then, with plain yet beautiful speech, the preacher exalted Jesus. Here was the Lamb of God for us to behold! Here was the sacrifice anticipated in the Old Testament and executed in the New. Here in Jesus was redemption. The sinless Son of God had indeed come into the world to save everyone who believes—even a former Muslim who was an avowed and determined enemy of the cross!

"Repent and believe for the forgiveness of your sins" came the invitation. In lavish kindness, God turned my wife and me from our sins and to Jesus in faith on that day. Literally overnight, God mercifully broke the stranglehold of years of anger and hatred. The gospel triumphed where no other power had or could. The gospel of Jesus Christ freed me from the clutches of sin and the darkness of Islam.

The gospel is the power of God for salvation to everyone who believes. I saw that power on the young Iranian woman's face that day. I've seen that power displayed in the faces of people from Muslim backgrounds in America and the Middle East. I've experienced and received that power myself through faith in Christ.

And I trust that this same gospel in your hands will produce the same conversion and new life in the Muslim people the Lord places in your path. This is why this book was written: to encourage ordinary Christians in the extraordinary power of the gospel.

Part One

The Gospel

God
by Any Other Name?

If a Muslim believes one thing, he or she believes that there is but one God. In fact, that's the cardinal confession of Islam: "There is only one God, and Muhammad is his messenger."

A Muslim child may have that confession recited over him or her thousands and thousands of times before the child is even able to speak. And the first act of converts to Islam is to make this confession: "There is but one God . . ."

For the Muslim, the radical unity of God—that there is only one God with no partners and no parts—sets Islam apart from all the pagan religions of the world. The highest blasphemy in Islam is *shirk*, associating others with or making others partners with God. To the Muslim mind, nothing could be more foul and dishonoring to God.

When I converted to Islam, the simple and radical unity of God was a very appealing doctrine. Like many people, I struggled with the complexities of the Trinity. How could God be one and yet three Persons? And how could one of the Persons of the Trinity, Jesus, be both fully God and fully human? The Trinity defied comprehension, and Islam offered a view of God conformable to human reason.

EMBRACING THE MYSTERY

Today, the Christian's task of proclaiming the gospel and persuading their Muslim neighbors and friends depends, in part, on faithfully embracing the mystery of the Trinity— God the Father, God the Son, and God the Holy Spirit. Many Christians have a slippery grip on this cardinal doctrine of the faith, and it makes for rather uneasy discussions with our Muslim friends. But what could be more appropriate than that we should stand in awe of God, overwhelmed not only by His acts but by His very person? After all, *He is God*.

Why should the litmus test for our view of God be human reason when both Muslims and Christians agree that God is infinitely above all that we can imagine or think? How could we ever know God unless He stooped to reveal Himself to us?

So from the outset, any discussion of God requires a certain humility. This is why James exhorts his readers to "humbly accept the word planted in you, which can save you" (James 1:21). We could never know God unless He revealed Himself to us. And if that's the case, embracing *whatever* He reveals of Himself is both necessary and humbling.

REVEALED RELIGION

Both Islam and Christianity are revealed religions. That is, they both depend on sacred texts wherein God discloses Himself and His will to mankind. So both the Muslim and the Christian should be in a receiving posture when it comes to identifying the character and work of God. They receive from God's hand what God desires them to know.

That raises a very important question. How are Christians to think of the Quran, and how are Muslims to think of the Bible?

For the purposes of explaining and applying the good news of Jesus Christ to our Muslim neighbors and friends, Christians don't have to spend a lot of time attacking the Quran.[1] Instead, our focus should be on helping our Muslim friends understand why they should humbly accept the Bible as revelation from God and therefore believe its message.

In God's marvelous kindness to Muslims and to Christians doing the work of evangelism, the Quran itself states ample enough reason for the Muslim to accept the Bible. In several places, the Quran affirms parts of the Bible as revelation from God. Those key passages, coupled with eagerness among many Muslims to try and refute the Bible, are enough to lead the conversation onto biblical and gospel-fertile soil.

The Quran teaches, for example:

No just estimate of Allah do they make when they say: "Nothing doth Allah send down to man (by way of revelation)." Say: "Who then sent down *the Book*

which Moses brought?—a light and guidance to man
(Sura 6:91, all italics added).

And it is your Lord that knoweth best all beings that
are in the heavens and on earth: We did bestow on
some prophets more (and other) gifts than on others:
and We gave to David (the gift of) the Psalms (Sura 17:55).

The Great Terror will bring them no grief: but the
angels will meet them [with mutual greetings]: "This
is your Day, . . . [the Day] that ye were promised." The
Day that We roll up the heavens like a scroll rolled up
for books [completed], . . . Even as We produced the
first creation, so shall We produce a new one: a promise We have undertaken: truly shall We fulfill it. *Before
this We wrote in the Psalms, after the Message (given to
Moses):* "My servants the righteous, shall inherit the
earth" (Sura 21:103–105).

*And in their footsteps We sent Jesus the son of Mary, con-
firming the Law that had come before him: We sent him the
Gospel: therein was guidance and light, and confirmation of
the Law that had come before him: a guidance and an
admonition to those who fear Allah. Let the people of the
Gospel judge by what Allah hath revealed therein"*
(Sura 5:46–47).

The first quote addresses pagan unbelievers who do not
believe God has spoken. The proof brought forward in the
Quran is not the Quran itself but "the Book which Moses

brought . . . a light and guidance to man." In other words, the Torah or Pentateuch, the first five books of the Bible, is offered as reliable proof to pagans and to Muslims of God's sending down divine revelation. So, those books should be acceptable and sufficient ground for evangelistic discussions with Muslims.

And notice in the last quote (Sura 5:47) that "the people of the Gospel" are told to judge all things by what is put in the Gospels. Six hundred years after Christ, the Quran records that even the prophet Muhammad understood and taught that the Gospels were reliable at arriving at the truth. Sura 10:94 reads: "If thou wert in doubt as to what We have revealed unto thee, then *ask those who have been reading the Book from before thee: the Truth hath indeed come to thee from thy Lord: so be in no wise of those in doubt"* (see also 16:43; 21:7). Here is a Quranic admission that the Bible is sufficient for matters of faith and conduct, requiring Muslims not to be among "those in doubt" about this fact.

> IF OUR MUSLIM FRIENDS
> *are consistent with their own teachings,*
> *they must accept the Torah . . . and the*
> *Gospels as . . . revelations from God.*

If that were not enough to establish the Bible's reliability as revelation from God, throughout the Quran Muslims are taught that "There is nothing that can alter the words of God" (6:34; 10:64; 18:27). According to the Quran, Allah promises to watch over the revelation and guard it from corruption (15:9).

As Christians, we know that these sentiments find their

expression in the Bible first. "Your word, O Lord, is eternal; it stands firm in the heavens" (Psalm 119:89; see 1 Peter 1:24–25). And Jesus taught, "It is easier for heaven and earth to disappear than for the least stroke of a pen to drop out of the Law" (Luke 16:17), and "Heaven and earth will pass away, but my words will never pass away" (Matthew 24:35).

If our Muslim friends are consistent with their own teachings, they must accept the Torah, the Psalms of David, and the Gospels as uncorrupted revelations from God. In our evangelism, the point is not to concede that the Quran itself is inspired revelation from God, but to lovingly push our Muslim neighbors and friends to the logical conclusion the Quran requires—the Bible is trustworthy revelation from God.

We can have complete confidence that the Bible when read and applied in the power of the Holy Spirit will accomplish God's saving plan. "As the rain and the snow come down from heaven, and do not return to it without watering the earth and making it bud and flourish, so that it yields seed for the sower and bread for the eater, so is my word that goes out from my mouth: It will not return to me empty, but will accomplish what I desire and achieve the purpose for which I sent it" (Isaiah 55:10–11).

The critical question for Muslim neighbors to consider and for Christians to press is, "What then does the Bible reveal about God that we should humbly accept?"

COMMON GROUND

Some things are not in dispute between Muslims and Christians when it comes to many of the attributes of God.

Muslims cheerfully agree with Christians that God is sovereign, omniscient, omnipotent, merciful, just, holy, righteous, benevolent, and so on. Both groups maintain belief in the moral perfections of God. And both groups believe that there is only one God.

There are at least two implications of this substantial agreement. First, the Muslim and the Christian stand in the same relationship to God as Creator to creature. We both acknowledge the unassailable right and reality of God's rule, and our duty to Him as His creatures.

Second, then, we both acknowledge that all mankind will have to give an account to God for our lives on earth. And because God is morally perfect, He will judge all unrighteousness and punish the wicked. We can then talk with one another as people with a sobering, vitally important question in common: How will anyone be reconciled to God and enter His presence?

The answer to that question is inextricably connected to who God reveals Himself to be. In other words, the doctrine of God and the Person of God cannot be divorced from the work of salvation. And this is where Muslims and Christians divide and where Christians must hold fast to the Trinity.

A ROSE BY ANY OTHER NAME?

A few years after leaving Islam and embracing Jesus Christ as Savior and Lord, I had the privilege of visiting my hometown for a debate with local Muslims. The organizers planned the roundtable discussion focused on the questions Who is God? and What is He like?

An hour into the discussion, we were getting nowhere. One of the participants continually avoided discussing the differences in Islam and Christianity by proclaiming, "We serve the same God. It's the same God with different names."

I confess. I was frustrated with that glib and unhelpful response. I wish that I had been more patient and more biblical in my attitude, but my retort seemed to drive the point home. I turned to this gentleman whom we'll call "Rahim," and said, "Pardon me, *Tony*."

He looked befuddled for a moment and said, "Excuse me?" I replied again, "Excuse me, *Tony*," waiting for Rahim to answer me.

He looked out at the audience as if to say, "What's going on here?" I pressed on, looking directly into Rahim's eyes, and asked, "*Tony*, could you please pass me that Bible on the chair in front of you?"

Now Rahim was frustrated and said, "Man, my name is not Tony. It's *Rahim*."

To which I replied, "If you expect to be properly addressed and known for who you are, why do you think God is okay with being addressed by any name and defined by those who call upon him?"

I wish I hadn't let frustration ruin my tone at that point. I wish I had been more patient and charitable. I don't recommend engaging anyone in this way. Instead, we should speak the truth in love. Sometimes we have to draw sharp lines in order to be understood—the debate moved on with much more substantive engagement from that point. But even when we draw lines, we should do so with love because we're representing a loving God we wish to make known.

CALL ON THE NAME OF THE LORD

Throughout the Bible, calling upon the name of the Lord is synonymous with receiving His salvation. We find Abraham calling on the name of the Lord (Genesis 12:8; 13:4; 21:33) after the Lord revealed Himself to Abraham (then Abram), made promises to Abram, and delivered Abraham from troubles. Later, Israel, the elect nation of God in the Old Testament, was "called by the name of the Lord" by all the peoples of the earth (Deuteronomy 28:10).

The psalmist pictures the saving deliverance of God as a response to calling on the name of the Lord.

> *The cords of death entangled me,*
> *the anguish of the grave came upon me;*
> *I was overcome by trouble and sorrow.*
> *Then I called on the name of the Lord:*
> *"O Lord, save me!"*
> *I will lift up the cup of salvation*
> *and call on the name of the Lord.* (Psalm 116:3–4, 13)

The prophet Joel foresaw a day of great and terrible judgment, when only those who call upon the name of the Lord would be saved (Joel 2:31–32). The prophets Zephaniah (3:8–10) and Zechariah (13:8–10) foresaw similar judgments and pictured escape or salvation in precisely the same terms— "they will call on the name of the Lord."

It's no surprise, then, that the New Testament writers picture salvation as calling upon the name of the Lord. The apostle Peter, in the first recorded sermon in the early church, quotes the prophet Joel (Acts 2:14–21) and applies his message directly to the life, crucifixion, and resurrection of Jesus Christ as "both Lord and Christ" (vv. 21–38). In Acts 4, Peter contended that it was by "the name of Jesus Christ of Nazareth" that a crippled man was healed, and that "salvation is found in no one else, for there is no other name under heaven given to men by which we must be saved" (Acts 4:10–12). The apostle Paul also quotes Joel 2:32 when he writes to the church in Rome and says, "Everyone who calls on the name of the Lord will be saved" (Romans 10:13), explicitly equating calling on the name with salvation from sin and judgment for Jew and Gentile alike.

But to "call on the name" does not narrowly mean Jesus Christ of Nazareth. It certainly includes that, but it includes more. In the Great Commission, the Lord Jesus Himself charges His disciples with making other disciples, in part, by baptizing them "in the name of the Father and of the Son and of the Holy Spirit" (Matthew 28:19). Notice that "name" is singular in this verse. The name of God most fully is Father, Son, and Holy Spirit.

To call upon the name of God is to call fully upon the Godhead, the blessed Trinity, one God in three Persons.

WHY SHOULD CHRISTIANS
CLING TO THE TRINITY?

Why does all this matter? Why should Christians make a fuss over God being one God in three Persons? Why not just focus on Jesus and avoid the difficulties of talking about the mystery of the Trinity? Or why not settle for the use of the term "God" and allow the listeners to fill it with whatever meaning is comfortable for them?

There are many reasons. But I think it's important to keep at least three in mind.

First, because we are bound in humility to accept what God reveals of Himself. After all, we are creatures and He is the Creator; we are finite and He is infinite. Accepting and maintaining the Trinity as central to the Christian faith is to say to God, "I believe *You*—not others and not myself—as You reveal Yourself." In short, believing and defending the Trinity is essential to genuine Christian faith and witness.

Second, because to deny the Trinity is to commit idolatry. Here the Christian and the Muslim come to irreconcilable differences. We may not maintain that God is one God in three Persons and at the same time accept that God is radically one with no persons in the Godhead as Muslims believe. That would be to accept a contradiction. And it would be to deny the revelation God gives of Himself, making an idol graven with the tools of our own imagination. God is jealous for His name. He calls His people to "worship [Him] in spirit and in truth" (John 4:24). Surrendering the Trinity turns us away from true spiritual worship of the only living God to idolatry.

> IF WE SURRENDER *the Trinity . . . we in effect deny the gospel.*

Third, we must cling to the Trinity because apart from the Father, Son, and Holy Spirit, there is no possibility of eternal salvation. If we surrender the Trinity, or weaken our presentation

of who God really is, we in effect deny the gospel. Each
Person in the Godhead plays an essential part in redeeming
sinners from judgment and bringing them to eternal life.
Consider the roles of each:

+ *God the Father* "chose us in him (Christ) before the
  creation of the world to be holy and blameless in his
  sight. In love he predestined us to be adopted as his
  sons through Jesus Christ, in accordance with his
  pleasure and will—to the praise of his glorious grace,
  which he has freely given us in the One he loves"
  (Ephesians 1:4–6). Apart from the Father's election
  and predestination, there is no rescue of sinners.

+ *God the Son* provides our "redemption through his
  blood, the forgiveness of sins" (Ephesians 1:7). Apart
  from the sinless sacrifice of the Son of God, God the
  Son, there would be no satisfactory atonement for
  sin (Romans 3:21–25a) and no way for sinful men to
  enter the presence of a holy, righteous, and just God
  (Hebrews 2:17–18). "Without the shedding of blood
  there is no forgiveness" (Hebrews 9:22). The God-
  man Jesus Christ offers the only sacrifice without
  blemish that is able to purify us and satisfy the
  Father.

+ *God the Holy Spirit* produces in the sinner the marvelous work of the new birth (John 3:3, 5–8). God
  the Holy Spirit becomes for the believer the "seal"
  and "a deposit guaranteeing our inheritance until
  the redemption of those who are God's possession—
  to the praise of his glory" (Ephesians 1:14). The

Spirit of God preserves us until the day of our complete redemption, when we shall be ushered into the presence of God and be satisfied with seeing His face (Psalm 17:15).

THE ONLY TRUE GOD

My debate colleague in my hometown called upon the name of Allah. In calling that name, he was not simply calling upon God in a different language. While it is true that the term "Allah" means "god" and is used by both Arab Christians and Muslims, what each group *means* by that name could not be more radically different. When the Muslim calls on the name of Allah, though he is sincere, he calls upon a name that cannot hear and that cannot save.

The Bible defines eternal life very clearly as knowing the only true God and Jesus Christ whom God has sent (see John 17:3). When the Christian calls on the name of the Lord, she or he calls upon the only name given under heaven where salvation may be found (see Acts 4:12).

Muslims and Christians agree that God is holy, just, righteous, and our judge. But our Muslim friends do not understand that that holy, just, and righteous Judge is none other than the Father, Son, and Holy Spirit. Unless they come to see this, they will enter eternity and be stunned with eternal grief to find waiting there the Son of God whom they rejected in this life.

What's in a name? When it comes to spiritual matters, everything! For only those who call upon the name of the Lord—and mean the Father, Son, and Holy Spirit—will be saved. This is the name we wish for our Muslim friends to call upon in faith and thus be saved.

My Christian friend, be humble and confident in what the Lord has revealed of Himself. He has told us what He is like—one God in three Persons, Father, Son, and Holy Spirit. And He has told us that eternal life depends upon knowing Him for who He is. We have come to know God through faith in His Son. Now we hold fast to what we have received so that we may introduce others to the Triune God who alone gives life.

Things *to* Remember

1. Muslims and Christians largely agree about the basic attributes of God (holiness, justice, etc.). This provides a friendly starting place for discussions.

2. The Christian view of the Trinity is essential to any notion of salvation from sin and judgment. We accept the Trinity ultimately because God reveals Himself to us in the Bible as one God in three Persons. Since Islam is a revealed religion that affirms the Torah, the Psalms of David, and the Gospels, intellectually honest Muslims must also accept the revelation of God's Triune nature. We could not know God except He has revealed Himself to us in His Word. Be confident that He is who He says He is.

2

Man's Sin:

Resting Lightly on the Muslim Conscience

Every so often my family tries to surprise me. But usually I'm able to spoil surprise gifts before they're given ... or can play the stoic when I didn't guess beforehand.

It's a bad habit, really. I wouldn't recommend it. It frustrates my wife come gift time. And my youngest daughter has taken on some of this tendency. I fear she will miss a lot of the wonder that really is in life because her father is such a curmudgeon.

Sometimes, though, I am surprised by the unexpected —as I was at two recent debates with Muslim apologists. In both instances, a questioner raised the issue of man's creation and the existence of sin. And in both cases, my jaw fell into my lap at the responses my Muslim counterparts gave to the question.

In the first debate, the Muslim apologist asserted that Christians did not understand the Genesis account of Adam and Eve's creation. He insisted that Adam—and for that matter, no prophet of God—had ever sinned. "They may have made some mistakes," he conceded, "but the prophets are free from sin."

Even half the predominantly Muslim audience leaned back in wonder.

In the second debate, the young Muslim squirmed as he explained that God does not require perfection from us because He made us with a serious flaw. Again, a pensive hush fell over the crowd as they pondered the implications of this statement. I asked for clarification. "Are you saying that God made us sinners?"

Again the squirming. "I'm saying," he replied, "that it is unfair for God to make us this way and expect perfection from us. Therefore, God must not expect perfection from people He made this way."

RESTING LIGHTLY ON
THE MUSLIM CONSCIENCE

The responses from these two Muslim speakers reveal significant differences between Muslims and Christians in their view of humankind. While Muslims and Christians agree that man is a created being who owes worship and obedience to God, they differ in their view of man and sin in several ways. In order to communicate the gospel and a person's need to embrace the Savior, Christians need to understand these differences.

Here are four questions about our humanity that a Christian and a Muslim would answer differently.

ARE PEOPLE CREATED IN
GOD'S IMAGE AND LIKENESS?

Christians believe that God created humanity in His own image and likeness (Genesis 1:26–27). Consequently, humanity uniquely reflects something of the glory of God. Humankind, both male and female, forms the apex of God's creation, endowed with capacities that separate them from the remainder of creation. Being made in God's image invests mankind with immeasurable dignity and provides the basis for social ethics ranging from our speech to one another (James 3:10–11) to prohibitions against murder and the use of judicial death sentences (Genesis 9:5–6).

Muslims reject the idea that man is made in the image and likeness of God. Islam teaches that Allah is wholly other than his creation. Nothing in creation shares Allah's glory or likeness. And in contrast to being found "good" at his creation, the Quran teaches that man was made with a weakness (Sura 4:28).

WHERE DOES SIN ORIGINATE?

Muslims and Christians also differ on the origin and meaning of sin. The Bible teaches that Adam, who represented all of humanity, committed the first sin when he broke God's command not to eat of the tree of the knowledge of good and evil (Genesis 2:16–17; 3). When Adam committed that sin, all of humanity fell into sin with him. "Sin entered the world through one man, and death through sin, and in this way death came to all men, because all sinned" (Romans 5:12). The Bible goes on to report that "consequently . . . the result of one trespass was condemnation for all men" and "through the disobedience of the one man the many were made sinners" (Romans 5:18–19).

Adam's disobedience produced several tragic consequences. First, Adam's sin introduced death into the world as the penalty of sin. Second, Adam's sin plunged all of humanity into sin with him and into God's condemnation of all men as well. Third, Adam's sin profoundly corrupted the nature of mankind, so that man not only sins but is a sinner. In fact, man is not a sinner because he sins, he sins because at his root he is a sinner. Sin is not only what we do, it is who we are. And for this reason, the Bible teaches that man is a slave to sin (Romans 6:6, 15–20; 7:25).

But the Islamic view is quite different. The Muslim account of man's creation does not include any significant emphasis on Adam's fall or the fall of all humankind into sin with Adam. Adam is not said to have sinned against God but to have made an ethical mistake. Muslims consider unjust the idea that one person's sins should be accounted to another person in any way. The Quran teaches that "no liability of one soul can be transferred to another" (Sura 6:164; 17:15; 35:18; 53:38).

So Muslims deny original sin. Most define sin as simply disobeying Allah's will. This disobedience comes from man's weakness and ignorance, but not from a corruption in his nature. Though Muslim scholars and clerics disagree on how to define the categories, Muslims do believe in minor and major sins.

DOES SIN OFFEND GOD?

Another way Christians and Muslims differ in their understanding of sin has to do with the object of sin. Who is sinned against? Chawkat Moucarry helpfully summarizes the Islamic understanding when he writes, "Islam teaches that our sins cannot offend our Creator, who stands too far above us to be directly concerned by our disobedience."[1] The Quran maintains that the person who sins "does evil to himself" (Sura 65:1).

But the Bible teaches that our sin is against God Himself. In our sin and sinful nature, we prove ourselves to be hostile toward God, alienated enemies to God (Romans 5:10; Colossians 1:21). Our sin personally affronts God. King David could say after his adultery with Bathsheba, "Against you, you only, have I sinned and done what is evil in your sight" (Psalm 51:4). Far from being dispassionately unmoved by sin, God is grieved by our sins (Genesis 6:5–6). And in His justice, God promises that He will not leave sin unpunished (Exodus 34:7), not even *unintentional* sins (Leviticus 4).

HOW SERIOUS IS SIN?

Given what we've covered already, we're not surprised that sin is significantly less serious in the Muslim view than the Christian. Sin rests lightly on the Muslim conscience because Muslims view sin primarily as weakness not wickedness, as general transgression not ungodly treason, and fail to see how it dishonors God precisely because it occurs in and through those made in God's image. But sin is such a terrible offense against God that the only thing that could assuage His holy anger toward us is the sacrifice of His only Son (Romans 3:25).

This means that one of the primary tasks Christians have in sharing the gospel is demonstrating the seriousness of sin for all people.

✗ BECOMING AWARE OF MY SIN

In my own conversion, the Lord used an office water cooler conversation to awaken me to my sin. A group of colleagues and I were discussing who among various people commanded our respect and admiration. Most of my colleagues listed great persons like Mahatma Gandhi and Martin Luther King Jr.

One colleague, a classmate from college, surprised me when she responded in all seriousness, "I can't think of anyone I respect more than Thabiti." Certain she was joking and perhaps sinfully flattering me, I protested with a dismissive wave of the hand and asked who she really admired. She insisted that I was more righteous than anyone she knew.

The word "righteous" fell into my empty heart, clanging and echoing against the walls of my soul. Instantly, I knew that I was not righteous. She commended me for not living a worldly life and treating my wife well, which were true enough. But I knew my own thoughts, my lustful desires, the hatreds that poisoned my heart. I knew in no uncertain terms that "righteous" was not a standing I held before God. The problem of my sin and unrighteousness dawned on me for the first time that day. My sin was a problem. My lack of righteousness was a problem. With this awareness, I began to realize that I needed a solution for my sin problem.

It's wonderful how the Lord uses passing conversations to make a lasting impact. A simple chat about "good" men and women struck my conscience.

HAVING "ALL THE RIGHT ANSWERS"

Often Christians place incredible pressure on themselves to have "all the right answers" and to say "just the right thing." I often think that that kind of pressure is a mixture of godly desire to help others and a serious lack of faith in God's ability to use what we *do* know to minister to others. Consequently, many Christians never begin to reach out to their Muslim neighbors and friends. We doubt our own ability and doubt that God can use us.

We may fail to realize that conviction of sin is God's work (John 16:8). He is pleased to ordinarily use people like you and me. But, ultimately, the Holy Spirit takes responsibility for making people aware of their sin and its heinousness. All we need to do is be faithful to raise the topic of righteousness and sin, to discuss the issue openly and honestly. Sometimes a basic question such as, "What do Muslims think about sin and judgment?" may open the way. At other times describing true virtue in others may expose the corruption of a person's heart.

Through the Scriptures we know more about the Muslim

and all non-Christians than they know about themselves. For example, we know that "the wrath of God is being revealed from heaven against all the godlessness and wickedness of men who suppress the truth by their wickedness, since what may be known about God is plain to them, because God has made it plain to them" (Romans 1:18–19). In other words, God tells us that men "suppress the truth" about God in unrighteousness. They really know the truth of their godlessness and wickedness, and they really suppress it. Our task becomes to lift the hands of suppression so that what is really known may rise to the surface.[2]

Thus, in our evangelism to our Muslim friends, we are to draw out the knowledge of sin, unrighteousness, God, and judgment that God has already placed inside their hearts.

FOSTERING URGENCY ABOUT THE DANGER OF SIN

One thing we have to do in sharing the gospel with our Muslim friends and coworkers is call them to respond urgently to the danger and corruption of sin in their lives. As long as they believe that Allah is not affronted by their sin, motivation to repent and confess their sin will be lacking. They need to see that the Bible calls sin a rebellion against God, which incurs God's wrath.

John Piper captures something of the desperate urgency associated with our sin, the wrath of God against sin, and the danger of an eternal hell. This should be our heart as we share the glorious good news of the gospel with our Muslim friends:

I must *feel* the truth of hell—that it exists and is terrible and horrible beyond imaginings forever and ever. "They will go away into eternal punishment" (Matt. 25:46). Even if I try to make the "lake of fire" (Rev. 20:15) or the "fiery furnace" (Matt. 13:42) a symbol, I am confronted with the terrifying thought that symbols are not overstatements but understatements of reality. Jesus did not choose these pictures to tell us that hell is easier than burning.

I must *feel* the truth that once I was as close to hell as I am to the chair I am sitting on—even closer. . . . Its views were my views. I was a son of hell (Matt. 23:15), a child of the Devil (John 8:44) and of wrath (Eph. 2:3). I belonged to vipers' brood (Matt. 3:7), without hope and without God (Eph. 2:12). I must believe that just as a rock climber, having slipped, hangs over the deadly cliff by his fingertips, so I once hung over hell and was a heartbeat away from eternal torment. I say it slowly, eternal torment!

I must *feel* the truth that God's wrath was on my head (John 3:36); His face was against me (Ps. 34:16); He hated me in my sins (Ps. 5:5); His curse and fury were my portion (Gal. 3:10). Hell was not forced on God by Satan. It was His design and appointment for people like me (Matt. 25:41).

I must *feel* in my heart that all the righteousness in the universe was on the side of God and against me. I was corrupt and guilty through and through, and God was perfectly righteous in His sentence (Ps. 51:4; Rom. 3:4).[3]

Do you feel the truth and the horrors of hell when thinking of sharing the good news of God's salvation with others?
How often do you reflect on the reality that you were once
a child of hell destined for God's wrath? Even a popular verse
like John 3:16—now largely sentimentalized by shallow
views of God's love—tells us of an already pronounced condemnation that the entire world is under because of sin.

The horror and certainty of sin and hell must burden us
and motivate us to share the truth about sin and its heinousness with our Muslim friends who think lightly of sin and its
consequences. I agree with Piper when he writes, "If I do not
believe in my heart these awful truths—believe them so that
they are real in my feelings—then the blessed love of God in
Christ will scarcely shine at all."[4]

PRESSING THE POINT HOME

Nabil tells the story of his conversion from a Muslim
background to faith in Jesus Christ.[5] Many significant conversations preceded his conversion, but one discussion with
his friend Henry proved critical. Nabil was fascinated by
Jesus' words in Matthew 9:12–13. "It is not the healthy who
need a doctor, but the sick. But go and learn what this means:
'I desire mercy, not sacrifice.' For I have not come to call the
righteous, but sinners."

Nabil asked Henry if Jesus was only interested in the
sick. Henry, aware that Nabil's real problem was a sin problem, pressed home the point of Jesus' words. "We are all sick
with sin. If you think that because you keep a few religious
rules you are not a sinner, you are mistaken."[6] Nabil quickly

saw the seriousness of his sin and his need for a Savior.

I'm thankful for Henry's wisdom and presence of mind. Nabil was in danger of missing the true point of Jesus' words. But Henry seized the opportunity to make sin unavoidable for Nabil. He risked being seen as unkind or judgmental to love Nabil enough by telling him he was a sinner. No amount of religiosity and external performance would change that.

A couple of Christian friends and I sat in a circle with a group of six or seven young Muslim men from Arab and Indian backgrounds. The conversation began pleasantly enough. We had gathered with the hope of simply cultivating some friendship. But after the pleasantries of introductions were over, our Muslim friends launched right into debate mode. After reeling for a while, and trying to discover ways to keep the conversation more pleasant in tone, I began discussing the necessity of accepting Jesus' sacrifice as atonement for sin.

ONE YOUNG MAN *who had sat quietly the entire time sat up, astonishment written on his face.*

A couple of the gentlemen continued to challenge us. Weary and more than a little frustrated, I kept pressing home the fact that they were all sinners and in danger of hell and God's judgment. After a few exchanges, one young man who had sat quietly the entire time sat up, astonishment written on his face. "Wait a minute," he interjected. "Are you saying that we may be going to hell?"

"Yes," I said.

"Do you realize that we are Arabs? I am an Arab Muslim."

With as much tenderness and clarity as I could muster, I said, "Arab Muslims are not exempt from hell. Your sins condemn you before a holy God."

I think it was the first time he'd ever been told that or understood how serious sin is from God's perspective. Until that point, I think he'd thought hell was a problem for non-Muslims and non-Arabs. He needed the point pressed home.

As far as I know, he didn't repent and believe that day. But I pray that by God's grace the trowel of the gospel dug into the soil of his heart, and that God planted the imperishable seed that will lead to his rebirth.

As long as sin remains a non-Arab, non-Muslim problem for some of our friends, they are likely to view life with lackadaisical dullness. They must be shaken awake to realize the true horrors of sin, wrath, judgment, and eternal torment. Only then will they see how necessary and amazing the grace of God in Jesus Christ really is.

Things *to* Remember

1. Sin is more than a "mistake" or a "weakness." Sin is a personal rebellion against God for which the Muslim is accountable to God. All those who die in their sins, never having repented of them and sought forgiveness through faith in Christ, will be eternally judged for their sins. Remember to weep over the horror of sin and God's judgment.

2. In evangelistic discussions, make sin a personal matter rather than an "academic" idea. Press home the point of sin and guilt graciously but clearly.

Jesus Christ:

Fully God and
Fully Man

Witnessing isn't always easy. If you've tried to be faithful in sharing the good news of Christ with others, you no doubt have had some false starts and stumbles along the way. I'm certainly no exception.

In 2000, the Lord moved my family to the Washington, D.C., area. We were excited about living in a new city and saw it as an opportunity to take the gospel to new neighbors and friends. In particular, I envisioned hundreds of opportunities to speak to people about Jesus on the Metro train rides in and out of the city each day.

Boy, was I in for a rude awakening! It turns out that striking up conversations with most people on the Metro is a real no-no. People look at you with this offended look as if to say, "You're not from around here, are you? We don't do that."

So, in time, I slipped into the Metro rider routine of reading on the train. But I carried on a private campaign to be friendly to the odd passengers who actually thought you should speak to people on the train.

One morning during my forty-five minute commute, I noticed a Muslim man waiting on the train. Though he stood some distance from me on the platform, we entered the same car. From the corner of my eye, I noticed him making his way up to me as I sat to read the Bible. I was not in the frame of mind to engage with anyone—today I was in the typical Metro rider mode. *Besides*, I told myself, I *haven't had time to complete my quiet time with God this morning.* I just wanted to read my Bible.

Imagine my discomfort when on an otherwise entirely empty Metro train car, this man sat down immediately next to me! He clearly wasn't from around here.

In God's providence, the genealogy of Jesus in Matthew's gospel served as my reading for the morning. My Muslim neighbor peeped over and asked, "What are you reading?"

"The Bible," I replied, quietly hoping that would end the conversation.

"Are you a student of comparative religion?" he asked.

Having heard that question a hundred times, I knew what was coming. *Okay,* I said to myself, *brace yourself.* I could hear that famous boxing announcer building to a crescendo, *"Let's get ready to rumble!"*

But quietly, I replied, "No, I'm a Christian."

"What part of the Bible are you reading?" he asked.

"Matthew 1," I told him.

He made a few commonplace comments then asked,

"Do you mind if I take a look at your Bible?" Reluctantly I agreed.

In the thirty to forty minutes that followed, my new Muslim co-passenger protested that Matthew's Gospel and Luke's account were filled with contradictions about Jesus. He went on about the fact that Jesus was called the Son of God, but so were Adam, Israel, and others.

I WAS COMPLETELY *unprepared for such a frenetic match of Bible ping-pong on the D.C. Metro.*

"So," he concluded with an air of triumph, "the title 'son of God' doesn't really mean what you think it means."

Frankly, I was completely unprepared for such a frenetic match of Bible ping-pong on the D.C. Metro at 7:45 a.m.! Honestly, I'm not prepared for much of anything social at 7:45 a.m.! I barely got a word into the conversation. And those I did register were rather weak and unconvincing. The plain truth be told: He kicked my rear end on that train ride into town that morning.

WHAT REALLY MATTERS

Typically, if we're thinking about winning or losing debates with our Muslim neighbors, we've lost sight of what really matters. We're not engaged in a contest where points can be scored and win-loss records tallied, with the victor earning bragging rites.

When Jesus asked His disciples, "Who do you say I am?" (Matthew 16:15), He wasn't posing an interesting but

ultimately meaningless trivia question. He was asking a
question that divided and determined eternity for everyone.
Whether we spend eternity in heaven or in an agonizing hell
facing God's wrath depends on how we answer that question.

When sharing the gospel with Muslim neighbors and
friends, it's helpful to make it clear that knowing Jesus is no
matter for light, impersonal speculation or intellectual spar-
ring. This is a matter of eternal life and death.

GETTING TO JESUS

A lot of evangelism books help Christians with learning
how to turn ordinary conversations with friends to spiritual
topics and the question of Jesus.[1] But I have never had any
difficulty coming to the topic of Jesus in conversations with
Muslim men and women. In almost every case, the Muslim
is the one to raise the topic! Getting to Jesus could never be
easier in evangelism.

But once Jesus is raised in conversation, it's important
that Christians be able to explain the Bible's teaching about
who Jesus is and what He has done. In the next chapter, we
consider the question, "What has Jesus done?" In this chapter, we consider the question, "Who is Jesus?" and why it matters in our evangelism.

WHO IS JESUS?

We shouldn't be surprised that many people do not
know how to answer the question, "Who is Jesus?'" In Jesus'
own day, rival theories about His identity circulated among

the people. When Jesus asked His disciples who the people thought He was, they answered, "Some say John the Baptist; others say Elijah; and still others, Jeremiah or one of the prophets" came the reply (Matthew 16:14).

But Jesus pressed the question with His own disciples, not allowing any equivocation on the matter. Peter responded, "You are the Christ, the Son of the living God" (v. 16). Peter's response has from the days of Jesus Himself been the clearest and simplest answer to the question, "Who is Jesus?" He is the Messiah, the Son of God.

God Himself testifies to this fact at Jesus' baptism, when the Father says, "This is my Son, whom I love; with him I am well pleased" (Matthew 3:17). The apostles, eyewitnesses to Jesus' life and ministry and unique messengers of Christ, testify that Jesus is the Son of God in their letters to the early church (for example, Romans 1:1–5; Hebrews 1:1–3; and 1 John 5:10–13). And in the strongest way possible, Jesus affirms Peter's confession that He is the Son of the living God by saying, "Blessed are you, Simon son of Jonah, for this was not revealed to you by man, but by my Father in heaven" (Matthew 16:17). In other words, Jesus does not refute Peter's claim but underlines the fact that Peter's confession came by divine revelation from God the Father. So true was Peter's claim that it could only be known by a supernatural act of revelation.

BUT WHAT IS MEANT BY "SON OF GOD"?

It's popular for Muslim apologists to admit that Jesus is the "son of God." But they do not intend by that admission to suggest that Jesus is God the Son. Rather, they maintain that the title "son of God" is used of several persons and even the entire nation of Israel. So, they contend, there is no reason to infer deity from this title. This was the argument my friendly Metro co-passenger wanted to stress on our train ride.

Of course, the Bible does use the title "son of God" to refer to persons other than Jesus. For example, Adam is called the "son of God" (Luke 3:38). Psalm 82:6 depicts God referring to another otherwise unnamed group as "sons of the Most High," and saying to them, "You are 'gods'" before He executes judgment against them. In Hosea 11:1, the entire nation of Israel is called "a child" and God's "son." And all Christians are referred to as sons of God (Romans 8:14; Galatians 3:26).

But the Bible uses the title "Son of God" in a unique way when referring to Jesus. Jesus is the "only begotten" or the "one and only" Son of God (John 3:16 NASB, NIV). He is not the Son of God because of the incarnation, or simply as a matter of title. He has *always* been and will always eternally be the Son of God in Person. So, Jesus prays in John 17, "Glorify your Son, that your Son may glorify you. And now, Father, glorify me in your presence with the glory I had with you before the world began" (vv. 1, 5). From eternity, Jesus shared the Father's glory as His only beloved Son.

Well, what about the other references to people and groups as "sons of God"? Those references point like veiled references to the coming of Jesus, the unique Son of God, God the Son. Adam "was a pattern of the one to come" (Romans 5:14). The "gods" or judges of Psalm 82 are replaced by Jesus the Judge in whom there is no corruption (John

5:26–30). And the nation Israel, as the son of God called out of Egypt, prefigures the true Son of God who fulfills even the pattern of Israel's exodus history in His own flight into Egypt (Matthew 2:13–15). Jesus Christ is the true Son who finally pleases the Father where all the other "sons" had failed. Adam introduced sin into the world; Israel continually turned from God to idols; but Jesus entered human history as the true Son of God and did all that the Father commanded.

When the Bible refers to Jesus as "the Son of God," we must recognize Jesus' absolute uniqueness. For in Jesus all the fullness of God dwells (Colossians 1:19). Jesus is "the image of the invisible God" and "the exact representation of his being" (Colossians 1:15; Hebrews 1:3), the Creator and Sustainer of creation (John 1:1–3; Colossians 1:16). This is what we mean when we say "Jesus is the Son of God." He is God the Son.

IS JESUS ONLY GOD AND NOT MAN?

Like discussions about the Trinity, discussions about the deity of Christ can appear very abstract and unnecessarily complex. In fact, many Muslims appeal to Christianity's complexity as their chief argument against the Trinity and the deity of Christ. Like one young man who asked me at a Christian-Muslim dialogue, "Wouldn't it be much simpler to say God is one and Jesus was just a man and messenger?"

Of course, it would be simpler. But it would not be true and it would not be the gospel. The efficacy of the gospel rests on the full deity and full humanity of Christ.

The writer to the Hebrews perhaps makes the most succinct case for the necessity of Jesus' full humanity.

Since the children have flesh and blood, he too shared in their humanity so that by his death he might destroy him who holds the power of death—that is, the devil—and free those who all their lives were held in slavery by their fear of death. For surely it is not angels he helps, but Abraham's descendants. For this reason he had to be made like his brothers in every way, in order that he might become a merciful and faithful high priest in service to God, and that he might make atonement for the sins of the people.
(Hebrews 2:14–17)

Keeping in mind that the writer of Hebrews opens the letter by stating that Jesus is "the radiance of God's glory and the exact representation of his being" (Hebrews 1:3), it's striking that he should now go on to emphasize Jesus' full humanity as well. Because Jesus offers Himself as our substitute, it was necessary that His life really be a human life since humanity owed the penalty of sin to God. So, Jesus took on our humanity to destroy Satan's work in our lives and liberate us. He had to be like us in every way so that He could serve as our faithful high priest and atone for our sins. And, indeed, Jesus has become our high priest, able to sympathize with us because He has carried our humanity, tempted like us in every way, yet without sin (Hebrews 4:15).

Since humanity transgressed God's commandments in sin, humanity needed to bear the penalty for sin. So it was necessary that Jesus be fully human, indeed perfect humanity, in order to satisfy the justice of God. "There is one God and one mediator between God and men, the man Christ Jesus" (1 Timothy 2:5).

The truth is, our salvation rests on both the full deity and the full humanity of Jesus Christ, the Son of God.

C. S. LEWIS AND OUR MUSLIM FRIENDS

Unlike the United States, Grand Cayman, where I live, has no considerable Muslim population. Most people here have no real interaction with Muslims or exposure to Islam. That's changing to some extent as the Islamic community grows, but talking with a Muslim is a rare event here.

So you might understand the community's surprise to learn that Muslims do not believe that Jesus is God's Son. For many of Cayman's people, a recent radio show provided the wake-up call.

The daily call-in talk-show host phoned to ask if I would speak on air with a Muslim caller who regularly phones in to share his views. After some discussion, I happily agreed.

Though the host wanted to have a very introductory discussion about the basic beliefs and differences of Islam and Christianity, the phone lines soon lit up as my counterpart asserted that Jesus was not God, only a prophet. He was stating a basic Islamic position, as Muslims seek to prevent any partners from being associated with Allah. But such clear opposition to Christian truth startled many listeners.

Muslims contend that they honor Jesus as a great prophet who performed miracles. But in response, Christians need to ask devout Muslims, "How can Jesus be a prophet who speaks the very words of God with miraculous signs and Muslims still deny what He taught about Himself?"

C. S. Lewis's now famous framework—Jesus is liar, lunatic, or Lord—makes the Muslim claim to honor Jesus completely unworkable. In *Mere Christianity* Lewis wrote:

> I am trying here to prevent anyone saying the really foolish thing that people often say about Him: "I'm ready to accept Jesus as a great moral teacher, but I don't accept His claim to be God." That is the one thing we must not say. A man who said the sort of things Jesus said would not be a great moral teacher. He would either be a lunatic—on a level with the man who says he is a poached egg—or else he would be the Devil of Hell. You must make your choice. Either this man was, and is, the Son of God: or else a madman or something worse. You can shut Him up for a fool, you can spit at Him and kill Him as a demon; or you can fall at His feet and call Him Lord and God. But let us not come with any patronizing nonsense about His being a great human teacher. He has not left that open to us. He did not intend to.[2]

To accept Jesus as a "good moral teacher" or as a prophet as Muslims do, only to then reject His prophecy and teaching is not an honest position to take. Jesus has not left that open to us. The Christian evangelist's task is to make the perfect deity and humanity of Christ an unavoidable reality for our Muslim friends. "Who is Jesus?" is the most important question ever asked. The correct answer is even more critical.

Things *to* Remember

1. Be sure to "get to Jesus" in your conversations with Muslims. Move the conversation to the critical question "Who is Jesus?"

2. Jesus is both the unique Son of God, God the Son and fully human. In the incarnation, God the Son takes on our nature so that He can offer Himself in our place.

Jesus Christ:

The Lamb Slain— and Resurrected!

The Kite Runner is a gripping coming-of-age novel about two young Muslim boys in soon-to-be war-torn Afghanistan. The book explores many of the cultural complexities of Afghani and Muslim culture. But the book's main theme is sacrifice. In one chapter, the main character, Amir, recalls the Muslim holiday where animal sacrifice takes central stage:

> Tomorrow is the tenth day of Dhul-Hijjah, the last month of the Muslim calendar, and the first of three days of Eid Al-Adha, or Eid-e-Qorban, as Afghans call it—a day to celebrate how the prophet Ibrahim (Abraham) almost sacrificed his son for God. Baba has handpicked the sheep again this year, a powder white one with crooked black ears.

We all stand in the backyard, Hassan, Ali, Baba, and I. The mullah recites the prayer, rubs his beard. Baba mutters, Get on with it, under his breath. . . .

The mullah finishes the prayer. Ameen. He picks up the kitchen knife with the long blade. The custom is not to let the sheep see the knife. Ali feeds the animal a cube of sugar—another custom, to make death sweeter. The sheep kicks, but not much. The mullah grabs it under its jaw and places the blade on its neck. Just a second before he slices the throat in one expert motion, I see the sheep's eyes. It is a look that will haunt my dreams for weeks. I don't know why I watch this yearly ritual in our backyard; my nightmares persist long after the bloodstains on the grass have faded. But I always watch. I watch because of that look of acceptance in the animal's eyes. Absurdly, I imagine the animal understands. I imagine the animal sees that its imminent demise is for a higher purpose. This is the look . . .[1]

This fictionalized account captures something of the tradition, meaning, and biblical basis for the Muslim holiday Eid-e-Qorban. But how prevalent is the theme of sacrifice in Islam?

DO MUSLIMS BELIEVE IN SACRIFICE?

In one sense, sacrifice provides a major motivation in Islam. It lies at the heart of the practice of hajj, or pilgrimage to Mecca. Ramadan, the Muslim month of fasting and prayer, calls upon faithful Muslims to sacrifice food and other comforts in religious devotion. The giving of alms provides opportunity to sacrifice for the poor.

But do Muslims understand the Christian idea of substitutionary penal sacrifice, one person standing in the place of another to pay the guilty person's penalty or debt?

The closest Muslims come to such a concept is the tradition of Eid-e-Qorban, where an animal is slaughtered in remembrance of Abraham's near sacrifice of his son—though Muslims believe Ishmael, not Isaac, was the potential sacrifice. While some authors think that Id offers a bridge between Christianity and Islam,[2] the Quran denies that animal sacrifice can atone for the sins of men. Speaking of the animals sacrificed during Id, the Quran states: "It is not their meat nor their blood, that reaches Allah: it is your piety that reaches Him: He has thus made them subject to you, that ye may glorify Allah for His Guidance to you and proclaim the good news to all who do right" (Sura 22:37).

In Islam, piety counts before Allah, not sacrifice.

AN IRRECONCILABLE DIFFERENCE

Muslims deny that Jesus is a penal substitutionary sacrifice. That is, they deny the Christian teaching that Jesus offered Himself as a substitute for our sins and a sacrifice who paid the penalty that all sinners owe for their transgressions. Does this denial amount to an irreconcilable difference with Christianity?

I think so. I've yet to hear a Muslim say, "You know what? What Christians teach about Jesus' death on the cross

reminds me of Eid-e-Qorban." In fact, after denial of the
Trinity, Christ's death as a sacrifice is perhaps the Christian
truth most strenuously opposed by Muslims. They find the
idea of an innocent man dying to atone for the sins of others
an abhorrent perversion of justice. And in denying that an
innocent man can justly take the place of a guilty man, our
Muslim neighbors and friends deny the central truth run-
ning throughout the Scripture.

GOD'S PROMISED SACRIFICE OF HIS OWN

The gospel is the story of God's sacrifice of His own
beloved Son in the place of hell-deserving sinners. It's a story
that God unfolds from the opening chapters of the Bible all
the way through to the climactic scenes of Revelation.

The sacrifice motif begins as early as Genesis 3:15. Immediately after Adam and Eve fall into sin, God curses the ser-
pent that tempted Adam and Eve. God promises that He "will
put enmity between you [the serpent] and the woman, and
between your offspring and hers; he will crush your head, and
you will strike his heel." Thus God makes the Bible's first
promise of a savior who will crush evil while suffering.

In His covenant promises to Abraham in Genesis 15, God
calls Abraham to supply a heifer, a goat, a ram, a dove, and a
pigeon. Abraham obeyed and cut the animals into halves.
Afterward, Abraham "fell into a deep sleep, and a thick and
dreadful darkness came over him." And while he slept, the
Lord appeared to him in a dream as "a smoking firepot with a
blazing torch" and passed between the pieces, vv. 15, 17. In
ancient covenants and treaties, ceremonies often included the

sacrifice of animals and a solemn pledge that should a party default on the terms of the covenant then the slaughter that happened to the animals should happen to them.[3] Abraham's dream was God's way of not only establishing a covenant with Abraham, but also of showing that His promises would be kept at the cost of sacrificing Himself.

Exodus 11–12 records the plague on the firstborn and the events of the first Passover during the exodus of Israel out of Egypt. Each household was to slaughter a year-old lamb and spread the blood of the lamb onto the doorposts of their homes. God promised, "The blood will be a sign for you on the houses where you are; and when I see the blood, I will pass over you. No destructive plague will touch you when I strike Egypt" (Exodus 12:13). Unlike the Quran's teaching about the sacrifices associated with Id, the blood of the Passover sacrifices did reach God and turn away His judgment.

> THE OLD TESTAMENT *prophets received the promise that God would make atonement for the sins of His people.*

The first seven chapters of Leviticus give detailed instructions for a variety of offerings that Israel was to make to the Lord. Unlike pagan sacrifices of the time, these offerings were made to atone for sin and guilt, not to appease whimsical and arbitrary deities. Israel's entire relationship with God was established by covenant, at the heart of which was a sacrificial system that provided a regular reminder of sin and transgression and atonement.

Even the Old Testament prophets received the promise that God would make atonement for the sins of His people. For example, the prophet Isaiah tells of a suffering servant who "was oppressed and afflicted, yet he did not open his mouth; he was led like a lamb to the slaughter, and as a sheep before her shearers is silent, so he did not open his mouth" (Isaiah 53:7). The suffering servant in Isaiah 53 would be "cut off from the land of the living;" the reason for his death: "for the transgression of my people he was stricken" (v. 8b).

And after a long and graphic depiction of Israel's spiritual adultery, for which they deserved God's judgment, the prophet Ezekiel recorded God's promise: "I will establish my covenant with you, and you will know that I am the Lord. Then, *when I make atonement for you for all you have done*, you will remember and be ashamed and never again open your mouth because of your humiliation, declares the Sovereign Lord" (Ezekiel 16:62–63; italics added). Just as pictured with Abraham in Genesis 15, here God promises that He—not the people—would make atonement for all their sins. The sacrifice would be His.

THE LAMB OF GOD REVEALED

All of these promises and prophetic pictures of sacrifice find their fulfillment in Jesus Christ. Matthew 1 includes the account of the angel of the Lord appearing to Joseph in a dream, instructing him to care for Mary because she was pregnant by divine intervention. Then the angel says, "She will give birth to a son, and you are to give him the name Jesus, because he will save his people from their sins" (v. 21).

From this episode we learn Jesus' very name is an indication that He had come to fulfill God's plan to rescue His people from their sins. But how would He do that?

John's gospel borrows the imagery of the Old Testament sacrificial system in a striking way. John the Baptist, on seeing Jesus, proclaimed, "Look, the Lamb of God, who takes away the sin of the world!" (John 1:29). The way Jesus would rescue His people from their sins would be to become God's own Lamb offered as a sacrifice in their place. All of the previous sacrifices simply pointed forward to this one sacrifice. The suffering servant of Isaiah 53 would be none other than Jesus, God's own Son. "With the precious blood of Christ, a lamb without blemish or defect," the sinner was to receive redemption (1 Peter 1:19). "Christ, our Passover lamb, has been sacrificed" (1 Corinthians 5:7).

And this is good news, indeed! As the writer to the Hebrews teaches, "The law requires that nearly everything be cleansed with blood, and without the shedding of blood there is no forgiveness . . . But now he [Jesus] has appeared once for all at the end of the ages to do away with sin by the sacrifice of himself" (Hebrews 9:22, 26b). Christ was sacrificed, we're told, "to take away the sins of many people" (v. 28).

If, like the fictional Amir in the novel *The Kite Runner*, who gazed into the eyes of the sheep, we could look into the eyes of the Lamb of God, we would see the look of acceptance. We would see in His eyes that the Lamb understood what He was doing. The Lamb saw His "imminent demise" and knew it was for a higher purpose—to redeem God's people from their sins.

And for His sacrifice, the redeemed will sing for all

eternity: "You are worthy to take the scroll and to open its seals, because you were slain, and with your blood you purchased men for God from every tribe and language and people and nation. You have made them to be a kingdom and priests to serve our God, and they will reign on the earth" (Revelation 5:9–10). Angels also will sing before the throne: "Worthy is the Lamb, who was slain, to receive power and wealth and wisdom and strength and honor and glory and praise!" (v. 12).

Muslims miss this glorious truth of God because they deny that Jesus sacrificed Himself for the sins of His people. They do not understand that the entire Bible focuses on God's sacrifice of His Son to redeem lost humanity.

AN OBJECTION: "IS THIS JUST?"

"But is this just?" That's the question that our Muslim friends ask when they hear the news that Jesus died in the place of sinners. It's not good news to them because they think it's not just for an innocent man to die in the place of the guilty.

Of course, Muslims are not the first to raise this objection. Six hundred years before Muhammad was born, many Jewish persons questioned whether the Christian view of atonement was just. That seemed to be part of the background conflict the apostle Paul addressed when he wrote to the church in Rome. Some of the Christians were struggling to understand how grace and justice could be reconciled. Some even went so far as to accuse Paul of teaching that the more unrighteous a person lived, the more God's righteousness was revealed, and that God would be unjust to show wrath (Romans 3:5). The apostle and his colleagues were being slandered with such mockeries of their teaching and of God's glory (Romans 3:7–8). But the apostle flatly denied these misrepresentations and errors.

To answer the objections of his opponents, the apostle Paul made this stunning claim: "God presented him [Jesus Christ] as a sacrifice of atonement, through faith in his blood. He *did this to demonstrate his justice*, because in his forbearance he had left the sins committed beforehand unpunished—*he did it to demonstrate his justice at the present time*, so as to be just and the one who justifies those who have faith in Jesus" (vv. 25–26, italics added).

Do you see what Paul is saying here? He is arguing that God *intentionally* presented Jesus as a sacrifice of atonement *to demonstrate His justice*. Jesus' sacrifice does not call God's justice into question; it demonstrates it! The cross is not a "problem" for the Christian; it is the solution to the charge that God is unfair!

By Jesus' sacrifice, God reveals and defends His justice in two ways. First, Jesus' suffering for the sins of His people

> JESUS' SACRIFICE
> *does not call God's justice into question; it demonstrates it!*

means that any sins unpunished beforehand are now fully punished in Christ. God leaves no sin unpunished. Mercy and grace do not come at the expense of justice. Second, because the sins of the faithful are fully punished in Jesus, God may justly declare righteous those who have faith in Jesus. That's what it means to be justified in God's sight—to be declared righteous by faith in Jesus. The cross, rightly understood, is God's own answer to any objection that He is unfair to substitute Jesus for the unrighteous.

HOW DO WE KNOW GOD IS SATISFIED WITH JESUS' SACRIFICE?

We know that God accepted Jesus' sacrifice on the sinner's behalf because God raised Jesus from the dead. The resurrection demonstrates that sin and death have been defeated at the cross.

The Lamb of God was slain but also raised to life so that those who believe in Him would live. Jesus puts it this way in John 11:25–26, "I am the resurrection and the life. He who believes in me will live, even though he dies; and whoever lives and believes in me will never die."

Princeton theologian J. Gresham Machen captured the beauty and wonder of both Jesus' sacrifice and His resurrection when he wrote:

> The atoning death of Christ, and that alone, has presented sinners as righteous in God's sight; the Lord Jesus has paid the full penalty of their sins, and clothed them with His perfect righteousness before the judgment seat of God.
>
> But Christ has done for Christians even far more than that. He has given to them not only a new and right relation to God, but a new life in God's presence for evermore. He has saved them from the power as well as from the guilt of sin.

The New Testament does not end with the death of Christ; it does not end with the triumphant words of Jesus on the Cross, "It is finished." The death was followed by the resurrection, and the resurrection like the death was for our sakes.

Jesus rose from the dead into a new life of glory and power, and into that life He brings those for whom He died. The Christian, on the basis of Christ's redeeming work, not only has died unto sin, but also lives unto God.[4]

The pivotal question in our evangelism is the question Jesus asked in John 11:26: "Do you believe this?" Do you believe that Jesus is the resurrection and the life and all who believe on Him will live forever? Do you believe that God accepted His sacrifice by raising Him from the dead and that all who believe in Him are brought into His life?

If you do, then you know an essential truth for sharing the gospel with your Muslim friends and associates. With confidence share this wonderful news with all your neighbors and friends! The Lord God Almighty has come, and He has sacrificed Himself and risen from the dead so that sinners may live!

Things *to* Remember

1. Jesus' sacrifice is both real and necessary. Apart from a sinless offering to God, no one can have their sins forgiven. Jesus' perfect sacrifice satisfies all of God's holy demands for atonement.

2. According to Romans 3:25–26, Jesus' sacrifice is the demonstration of God's righteousness. His death in our place is far from being unfair; it is how God demonstrates His justice and simultaneously declares the sinner righteous. Unless people trust in Jesus' sacrifice, they cannot be reconciled to God; they are still in their sins.

5

Response:

There's Repentance and Faith . . . and Then There Is Repentance and Faith!

The New York Times has a slogan on its masthead dating back to 1896: "All the News That's Fit to Print." We may not always agree on what's fit in a particular newspaper or magazine, however. For example, one edition of U.S. News & World Report included the following headlines:

FIVE RISKS ASSOCIATED WITH DIABETES MEDICATION

A FULL PLATE FOR CONGRESS: AL FRANKEN GIVES THE PARTY A FILIBUSTER-PROOF MAJORITY

ROMER: ECONOMIC CRISIS A WAKE-UP CALL

In the science section, there was an article entitled, "Plants Kept the Ice Age in Check." In education, one headline read, "Students Suffer Abusive Restraint, GAO Says."

I'm sure this is not "all the news that's fit to print," but it's a sampling of the people, places, and events deemed newsworthy that day. News reports feature interesting people, like comedian-turned-politician Al Franken. And those people are part of a story, an action narrative, like a worldwide economic crisis threatening homes and businesses that is abating slightly in 2010. Some of the stories have dramatic implications for people, like how to properly take diabetes medication.

News reports and advertisements saturate today's world. The average person gets bombarded with somewhere between 1,000 and 5,000 messages and advertisements per day! There is a lot of news vying for our attention.

THE GOSPEL: GOOD NEWS . . .
BUT ALSO DEMANDING NEWS

That means a lot of competition exists between the good news of Christianity and thousands and thousands of other news stories. The gospel of Jesus Christ has similarities and dissimilarities with other news reports. However, most people will pay more attention to the people, places, and events of the nightly television news programs than they will the good news of Jesus Christ crucified and resurrected for their souls.

The gospel, like other reports, features particular people, places, and events. It's the news of Jesus Christ, the Son of

God, who was born of a virgin, lived a sinless life, taught about the kingdom of heaven, performed miracles, was crucified and buried, and resurrected to purchase forgiveness and eternal life.

However, the gospel is also *unlike* other kinds of news. Other reports may be pondered and put off as inconsequential or irrelevant. But the gospel makes demands upon every person ever born. God "commands all people everywhere to repent" (Acts 17:30). Moreover, everyone must trust or believe in Jesus. "For God so loved the world that he gave his one and only Son, that whoever believes in him shall not perish but have eternal life. . . . Whoever believes in him is not condemned, but whoever does not believe stands condemned already because he has not believed in the name of God's one and only Son" (John 3:16, 18).

The gospel cannot be laid aside with yesterday's newspapers. Whether or not a person responds to the gospel appropriately—in repentance and faith—has implications for this present life and the life to come.

WHAT ARE BIBLICAL REPENTANCE AND FAITH?

The call to repent of sin and believe in the Lord Jesus Christ reverberates throughout the New Testament. We first hear the call to repentance and faith in the preaching of John the Baptist (Matthew 3:1–12). Jesus Himself, when He commences His public ministry, calls His hearers to repent and believe (Matthew 4:17; Mark 1:15). And the apostles after Jesus insisted that their audiences respond to the gospel in precisely the same way (Acts 2:37–38, 41; 26:20).

Theology professor Wayne Grudem offers a helpful definition of biblical repentance. "Repentance, like faith, is an intellectual *understanding* (that sin is wrong), an emotional *approval* of the teachings of Scripture regarding sin (a sorrow for sin and hatred of it), and a *personal decision* to turn from it (a renouncing of sin and a decision of the will to forsake it and lead a life of obedience to Christ instead)."[1]

Repentance basically means "to turn" intellectually, emotionally, and volitionally from sin to God. It involves turning away from the life of sin and idols and turning to God in faith. That's the response early church leaders commended when the gospel was preached. For example, that's how the apostle Paul recounts the events in Thessalonica:

> *The Lord's message rang out from you not only in Macedonia and Achaia—your faith in God has become known everywhere. Therefore we do not need to say anything about it, for they themselves report what kind of reception you gave us. They tell how you turned to God from idols to serve the living and true God, and to wait for his Son from heaven, whom he raised from the dead—Jesus, who rescues us from the coming wrath.* (1 Thessalonians 1:8–10)

True response to the gospel has not happened where repentance is lacking. One preacher described faith in Jesus without repentance as a hundred dollar bill with print only on one side. It may look like genuine currency, but what it lacks invalidates the whole.[2]

Like repentance, faith involves the entire person—his or her mind, emotions, and will. Faith is knowing the truth about Jesus Christ and what He has done for our salvation, accepting those facts with a joyful heart, and making a personal decision to trust Jesus to save you. The person who has faith or believes in Jesus Christ depends on Jesus to deliver him or her from the judgment of God against sin. Their confidence is in Jesus and not themselves for eternal life.

James Montgomery Boice provides a nice illustration of biblical faith from the life of missionary John G. Paton. A pioneer missionary to the New Hebrides Islands, when he arrived Paton discovered the natives had no way of writing their language. Boice writes:

> He began to learn [the language] and in time began to work in a translation of the Bible for them. Soon he discovered that they had no word for "faith." This was serious, of course, for a person can hardly translate the Bible without it. One day he went on a hunt with one of the natives. They shot a large deer in the course of the hunt, and tying its legs together and supporting it on a pole laboriously trekked back down the mountain path to Paton's home near the seashore. As they reached the veranda both men threw the deer down, and the native immediately flopped into one of the deck chairs that stood on the porch, exclaiming, "My, it is good to stretch yourself out here and rest." Paton immediately jumped to his feet and recorded the phrase. In his final translation of the New Testament this was the word used to convey the idea of trust, faith, and belief.[3]

Faith is stretching yourself out and resting upon Jesus and His work on the cross as the sole grounds for your right standing with God. Faith is turning to Christ as your only Savior and Lord. Together, repentance and faith make up what Christians generally refer to as "conversion."

REPENTANCE AND FAITH IN ISLAM

When we attempt to share the gospel with a Muslim friend, language can be an issue. I don't mean that we will be ineffective if we don't know Arabic. Rather, we must realize that Christians and Muslims often use the same terms with very different meanings. "Repentance" and "faith" are two examples.

Muslims use the term "repentance" to refer either to the conversion of non-Muslims to Islam (Sura 5:36–37) or of Muslims themselves turning to God (Sura 24:31). Men and women are called to repent because they are too weak to obey all of Allah's commands. Their repentance must be genuine in order to be acceptable to Allah (Sura 66:8), but it's unclear what things require repentance since Muslim theologians make a distinction between major and minor sins. All Muslims agree that repentance for major sin is necessary. But some say that minor sins do not require repentance.[4]

In Islam, faith may be defined in one of three ways, depending on the school of thought a Muslim supports. Faith may be defined simply as obeying the commands of God. Or, a Muslim may believe that faith includes both obedience and a profession of trust and belief in God. According to Sura 49:14, there are those who submit to Allah in obedience but nevertheless have not had faith or belief to enter their hearts. This introduces some confusion about the nature of faith in Islamic theology.

HOW TO MAKE THE BIBLICAL RESPONSE CLEAR

So when we're sharing the good news of Jesus Christ with our Muslim friends, it's important that we make a few things clear.

First, we must make it clear that all sin offends our holy God. Therefore all sins—even unintentional sins (see Leviticus 4)—require repentance and an atoning sacrifice. Moreover, specific sins are not fundamentally the problem; sin is. The existence and ugliness of the thing itself is the foundational problem, not merely its instances. Therefore, whether minor or major, sin and its expressions are always serious and the sinner is always in need of repenting.

Second, we must make it clear that genuine repentance requires abandoning sin. Repentance requires more than sorrow over "major" transgressions. Repentance requires we turn our backs completely on the old life of sin, that "with regard to [our] former way of life, to put off [our] old self, which is being corrupted by its deceitful desires; to be made new in the attitude of [our] minds" (Ephesians 4:22–23). Repentance is like crossing a bridge and burning it, so that we may never travel back to that path of sinful desires and habits again.

Third, we must make it clear that genuine faith requires accurate knowledge of, agreement with, and personal acceptance of what God has done for us in Jesus. Faith is not merely reciting the *shahada*, the Muslim profession that there is but one God and Muhammad is his messenger. Nor is faith merely praying the sinner's prayer or responding to an altar call, as some Christians believe. Faith is a gift from God wherein the sinner personally entrusts himself to Jesus as Lord and Savior who purchases forgiveness and eternal life through His crucifixion and resurrection. There is no saving faith that does not look to Jesus in this way.

Fourth, we must make it clear that forgiveness with God comes by grace alone apart from any works of righteousness. Genuine conversion issues forth in good works and a changed life (Ephesians 2:10), but good works and a moral life do not earn God's forgiveness or salvation. Muslims believe that good deeds are essential for earning salvation, being added to faith. But that's not the gospel of the Bible. Adding anything to the cross of Christ is slavery to the law and makes Christ "of no value to [us] at all." Depending on our righteousness alienates us from Christ and God's grace (Galatians 5:1–4).

To be effective in evangelism, we need to scrape the confusing and misleading barnacles off the Bible's teaching about repentance and faith. But is the difference merely semantic, merely a matter of word choice?

HOW TO USE BIBLICAL LANGUAGE TO DESCRIBE THE CHANGE WE SEE IN CONVERSION

The unique phrases and words of Scripture offer another way Christians can surmount the language problems we sometimes face with Muslims when describing conversion. For example, the phrase "born again" succinctly captures what Christians mean when we discuss conversion and sets that experience off radically from anything Islam describes. Though Muslims and Christians use such common terms as "repentance" and "faith," biblical words like "born again," "united to Christ," and "a new creation" communicate the very real differences between an Islamic and Christian understanding of conversion. So when we share the gospel, we should attempt to explain these differences in five areas.

First, we should explain that *to be a Christian is to be reborn.* Jesus says in John 3:3, "I tell you the truth, no one can see the kingdom of God unless he is born again." As one writer puts it, "What happens in the new birth is not getting new religion but getting new life."[5]

Second, we should explain that *to be a Christian is to be born of God.* Jesus elaborates on what it means to be born again when He says, "You should not be surprised at my saying, 'You must be born again.' The wind blows wherever it pleases. You hear its sound, but you cannot tell where it comes from or where it is going. So it is with everyone born of the Spirit" (John 3:7–8). In conversion, the sinner is born again by the sovereign work and power of God the Holy Spirit, who blows wherever He pleases. That is radically different from anything Islam teaches in its view of conversion. Such a conversion is not a human achievement. The Bible teaches, "All who received him, to those who believed in his name, he gave the right to become children of God—children born not of natural descent, nor of human decision or a husband's will, *but born of God*" (John 1:12–13, italics added). God does the work of producing new birth from the lives of people dead in sin.

Third, we should explain that *to be a Christian is to be*

raised from death to life. Romans 6:1–5 describes the resurrected life of conversion.

> *What shall we say, then? Shall we go on sinning so that grace may increase? By no means! We died to sin; how can we live in it any longer? Or don't you know that all of us who were baptized into Christ Jesus were baptized into his death? We were therefore buried with him through baptism into death in order that, just as Christ was raised from the dead through the glory of the Father, we too may live a new life. If we have been united with him like this in his death, we will certainly also be united with him in his resurrection.*

So radical is God's work of conversion or regeneration, it can only be likened to death and resurrection, dying to sin and living a new life for God.

Fourth, we should explain that *to be a Christian is to be spiritually united to Christ.* This is another biblical truth that helps to set Christian conversion apart from Islamic ideas of conversion. The Bible teaches that in conversion God unites the Christian to Himself through His Son. We have been "united with him" (Romans 6:5). The apostle Paul described the Christian experience when he wrote: "I have been crucified with Christ and I no longer live, but Christ lives in me. The life I live in the body, I live by faith in the Son of God, who loved me and gave himself for me" (Galatians 2:20). The Christian's life "is now hidden with Christ in God" (Colossians 3:3). This is the renewed life that we need and must have if we are ever to enter the kingdom of heaven.

Finally, we should explain that *to be a Christian is to be a new creation.* "If anyone is in Christ, he is a new creation; the old has gone, the new has come! All this is from God, who reconciled us to himself through Christ" (2 Corinthians 5:17–18a).

The change of conversion is radical, and using the radical language of the Bible is best for demonstrating the difference to our Muslim friends.

WHAT MAKES THE GOOD NEWS GOOD?

Once, during a public dialogue with Omar (not his real name), I was reminded how the gospel offers good news to all who believe in Jesus Christ. After taking the opportunity to present what our respective faiths taught about Jesus Christ and salvation, Omar and I sat across from one another for a period of question and answer. During his allotted time, he asked if I were certain I was going to heaven. I answered, "Yes."

When it was my turn to ask him questions, I asked the same. "Are you sure that you are going to heaven?"

With great confidence and a perplexing happiness, Omar said, "No. I cannot be sure I am going to paradise. It is possible for me to turn away from Islam. It is possible that I will be unrepentant of some sin and Allah will not let me enter paradise."

Omar gave a very honest answer. But in doing so, he revealed a major contrast between the Christian and Muslim conceptions of conversion and life with God. In the Muslim view, conversion is an essentially human-achieved status and paradise cannot be guaranteed. There is no assurance of Allah's forgiveness or of entering paradise.

In the Christian view, conversion and salvation are God's work from first to last. Because Jesus is our perfect sacrifice and our perfect righteousness, because He vicariously satisfies all that God requires of humanity, all those who trust in Jesus may be assured of God's forgiveness and of the gift of eternal life. And more than "outside" assurances, the Christian receives the internal testimony of God the Holy Spirit. For at the moment of our conversion, we "received the Spirit of sonship. And by him we cry, 'Abba, Father.' The Spirit himself testifies with our spirit that we are God's children. Now if we are children, then we are heirs—heirs of God and co-heirs with Christ" (Romans 8:15b–17a). The entire purpose for which God inspires certain portions of Scripture is to assure us of His love and forgiveness. The apostle John ends one of his letters with this purpose statement: "I write these things to you who believe in the name of the Son of God so that you may know that you have eternal life" (1 John 5:13).

The radical nature of the new birth, the testimony of Scripture, and the testimony of God the Holy Spirit assure the Christian of his acceptance with God the Father. Such assurance is not available for the Muslim, but it becomes good news for all who believe—including any Muslim who finds Jesus as his Savior.

How firm is this acceptance with God the Father? The Scripture says it is vouchsafed through the beloved Son of God, the Redeemer Jesus Christ (Ephesians 1:6–7). God Himself accomplishes and guarantees our salvation by His grace through faith in His Son. It depends on God, not man. This is why the gospel is *good* news, demanding a response from every person.

Things *to* Remember

1. Genuine repentance and faith require turning from the old life of sin lived apart from God and turning to God through faith in His Son. A person is saved by God's grace alone through faith alone apart from any works of righteousness. In our evangelism we must make these truths clear because Muslims use the same words with very different meanings.

2. One way to clarify the Christian understanding of conversion is to use uniquely Christian language, such as "born again," "rebirth," and "new creation."

Part Two

As You Witness

6

Be Filled
with the Spirit

Several years ago I attended an evangelism conference led by a popular Canadian evangelist of Indian descent. He was winsome, informative, and engaging. At one point, he asked the audience, "What do you think is the biggest hindrance to the spread of the gospel?"

It was a good question. At the time, I don't think I'd ever been asked the question so plainly. The audience responded with a lot of the usual reasons for failure in Christian evangelism: lack of opportunity, lack of knowledge, the poor examples of some "bad witnesses," hypocrisy in the church, and so on. But perhaps the most frequent example cited was fear.

Most people believed that fear of rejection, fear of reprisal, fear of being asked questions, and fear of failure hindered most Christians from sharing their faith with others. I think there is a lot of truth in their responses.

FEAR'S STRONG GRIP

Fear motivates or hinders a lot of behavior. We speak of being in the "grip" of fear. That's a wonderful metaphor because fear does tend to clasp us with strong hands and hold us in its sway. Fear grapples with us like an Olympic wrestler, securing us in a firm hold and pinning us to the mat.

I've felt the strong grip of fear. I once was invited to participate in a public dialogue with a Muslim apologist on the subject "Who is Jesus Christ and how are we saved?" It was a subject chosen by the Muslim students sponsoring the discussion. So you might expect that I would have few apprehensions. However, the night before public dialogue, I sat on the side of my bed overcome with fear. It had lurked around my heart for months, literally from the moment I received the invitation to come participate in the public dialogue. I don't know why I was so afraid. This would be my third such visit, and the previous two had gone really well. But I was panic-stricken.

In preparation for the discussion, I listened to an earlier debate featuring the young Muslim speaker I was soon to debate. During this earlier debate, the moderator asked the Muslim whether he thought converts from Islam who publicly made their conversion known should be killed. Without hesitation, he answered, "Yes, absolutely. If they speak of leaving Islam in a Muslim country, they may confuse and mislead weaker Muslims, causing others to doubt and disbelieve. To protect weaker Muslims, such a person should be killed."

In a few hours I would stand on the same platform with this man discussing the questions "Who is Jesus and how are we saved?" I imagined a few of the things that could go wrong. This was a Muslim city and a very public discussion. The larger the event, the less controlled the atmosphere could be. There could be an angry and perhaps even violent reaction to the fact that a former Muslim would now be recounting his conversion and sharing the gospel in a Muslim country. .

I've never been more afraid in my life. I picked up the phone and called my wife. I just wanted to hear her voice and pray. Fear suggested it might be the last time. And it suggested that a "wiser course" would be to play down my conversion when the time came. What happened? I'll take you to the debate at the end of the chapter.

THE PROBLEM WITH THE APOSTLE PAUL

We can learn about handling our fears from the apostle Paul. Look at the apostle and you may conclude that he faced every threat with boldness, zeal, and determination—and little fear. Reading some of his exploits in the book of Acts leaves you saying, "I wish I was more like that." And, "What a great Christian witness!"

The apostle Paul seems almost superhuman. And that's the problem with Paul. He stands as almost legendary to most Christians today.

But is that how things really were with Paul?

On one occasion, the apostle Paul described what he and his companions experienced in their missionary labors. "We do not want you to be uninformed, brothers, about the hardships we suffered in the province of Asia. We were under great pressure, far beyond our ability to endure, so that we despaired even of life. Indeed, in our hearts we felt the sentence of death" (2 Corinthians 1:8–9a). His admission certainly contradicts my overly romantic ideas about the apostle Paul.

It seems that the Christians at Corinth might have been under the wrong impression about Paul too. But the apostle makes it clear that at times Timothy and he felt themselves unable to endure the pressures of Christian life and ministry. They "despaired even of life." They "felt the sentence of death" in their hearts. They were in the grip of fear.

And this was not an unusual experience for Paul. The apostle's life was often in danger. He wrote to the Corinthian church about being imprisoned, whipped, and exposed to death. He gave many of the details in 2 Corinthians 11:24–27:

Five times I received from the Jews the forty lashes minus one. Three times I was beaten with rods, once I was stoned, three times I was shipwrecked, I spent a night and a day in the open sea, I have been constantly on the move. I have been in danger from rivers, in danger from bandits, in danger from my own countrymen, in danger from Gentiles; in danger in the city, in danger in the country, in danger at sea; and in danger from false brothers. I have labored and toiled and have often gone without sleep . . . I have been cold and naked.

Then he asked in summary, "Who is weak, and I do not feel weak?" (v. 29) The apostle knew suffering, weakness, and fear. He was not immune to the same temptations we face—

including fear. This is why he asks the Ephesian church to pray for him: "Pray also for me, that whenever I open my mouth, words may be given me so that I will fearlessly make known the mystery of the gospel, for which I am an ambassador in chains. Pray that I may declare it fearlessly, as I should" (Ephesians 6:19–20).

Paul was a man who put his sandals on one foot at a time just like the rest of us. He was not superhuman. And though his exploits for the Lord were great, he experienced all that we experience: fatigue, hunger, joy, pain, uncertainty, and even fear. That's why he asked others to pray for his boldness, to pray that he might be fearless when he spoke to others about the gospel of our Lord.

CAN FEAR AND BOLDNESS COEXIST?

Judging by the apostle Paul's life, we may emphatically conclude that "Yes, fear and boldness can coexist!" Boldness is not what people do when they are unafraid; boldness is what people do in the face of fear.

And boldness comes, in part, when we fear the appropriate Person—when we seek to love, revere, and stand in awe of God rather than men who may oppose us.

In Matthew 10, the Lord Jesus sent His disciples on a short-term mission trip. He warned them that they would face all kinds of opposition and persecution, even from their family members (vv. 17–22). The persecution would be so strong that Jesus described His followers as "sheep among wolves" (v. 16). It would be natural for His disciples to have a fearful response to the threat of bodily harm.

But the Lord reminded His disciples that they are not to be afraid of their enemies. "Do not be afraid of those who kill the body but cannot kill the soul. Rather, be afraid of the One who can destroy both soul and body in hell" (v. 28). In other words, a healthy fear of the Lord displaces the fear of men. This was King David's experience as he proclaimed, "In God, whose word I praise, in the Lord, whose word I praise—in God I trust; I will not be afraid. What can man do to me?" (Psalm 56:10–11).

There are limits to what men can do to us, but there is no limit to God's power. And the wonderful truth is that our omnipotent God uses His power for our welfare. "Are not two sparrows sold for a penny? Yet not one of them will fall to the ground apart from the will of your Father. And even the very hairs of your head are all numbered. So don't be afraid; you are worth more than many sparrows" (Matthew 10:29–31). If we fear the Lord, we remember that God is for us, watching over the details of our lives like a loving father watches over his children. We are worth more than many sparrows, seemingly insignificant parts of His creation which He tends all their lives. So, we need not be afraid of men. "The Lord is my light and my salvation—whom shall I fear? The Lord is the stronghold of my life—of whom shall I be afraid?" (Psalm 27:1).

WHERE DID PAUL GET HIS BOLDNESS?

Many people think of boldness as something they summon from somewhere down in their "gut." Athletes speak of "gut-check time" when the game is close and courage is needed. We commend a "gutsy performance" by an actor or actress who stretches himself or herself in a daring role. And we admire people who "have guts." We tend to think boldness comes from an internal store of strength and valor. Those who have it are able to flip a switch and exert it "when the chips are down."

It's all very cliché—and very inaccurate from a Christian perspective. When the apostle Paul asks the Ephesian Christians to pray for his boldness, it seems fairly clear that he doesn't imagine boldness to reside somewhere in his "guts." In fact, the prayer request suggests that the apostle is concerned about not having boldness at all when it comes to speaking about Jesus. Perhaps he had even failed to speak fearlessly on previous occasions, and so he knew the sting that comes from cowering when you should stand.

So where did Paul's boldness come from if it didn't come from within himself?

The boldness Paul needed and demonstrated came not from himself but from God the Holy Spirit. To witness effectively for Christ, we need to be filled with the Holy Spirit.

BE FILLED WITH THE HOLY SPIRIT

A lot of confusion exists about what the Bible means when it refers to being filled with the Holy Spirit. Some people imagine a "second work of grace" in the believer's life, so that some people have this "filling" and others do not. Some people think of being "filled with the Spirit" the way they think of filling a glass with water or punch. The Christian was "empty," and now a new "filling" happens.

When the Bible speaks of being "filled with the Spirit," a different picture comes to mind. Being filled with the Spirit means being controlled by the Spirit the way a boat's sails are filled with the wind and blown on its course. The Spirit gives power to the Christian so that the Christian may witness for Christ. That's the promise of Jesus in Acts 1:8— "*You will receive power* when the Holy Spirit comes on you; and *you will be my witnesses* in Jerusalem, and in all Judea and Samaria, and to the ends of the earth" (italics added). And when we read through the book of Acts, the activity most frequently associated with the Spirit's filling is speaking with boldness.

Consider the following:

+ In Acts 2:4, the apostles "were filled with the Holy Spirit and began to speak in other tongues as the Spirit enabled them." Peter explains that the miraculous gift of tongues fulfilled Joel's prophecy of a day when God's Spirit would be poured out on all flesh and people would prophesy. And Peter preached the gospel boldly to his Jewish audience and about three thousand souls were saved that day.
+ In Acts 4, Peter and John are arrested for teaching the resurrection of the dead. When they are brought before the rulers, elders, and high priest, Peter was filled with the Holy Spirit and spoke to them of Jesus' crucifixion and resurrection, and their guilt in the Lord's death. Verse 13 tells us that the religious leaders "*when they saw the courage* of Peter and John . . . they were astonished."

+ Later in Acts 4, when Peter and John are released from prison and share their story with the other disciples, they prayed that God would "grant to your servants to continue to speak your word with all boldness" (Acts 4:29 ESV). "And when they had prayed, the place in which they were gathered together was shaken, and *they were all filled with the Holy Spirit and continued to speak the word of God with boldness*" (Acts 4:31 ESV).

+ In Acts 6, Stephen defended the faith against a number of opponents of the gospel. While they resisted Stephen, "they could not stand up against his wisdom or the Spirit by whom he spoke" (v. 10). Though alone, Stephen spoke boldly in the power of the Spirit as Acts 7 records.

+ It was on his first missionary journey that the apostle Paul was filled with the Holy Spirit. He and Barnabas were opposed by a magician named Elymas (Acts 13:8). "Then Saul, who was also called Paul, filled with the Holy Spirit, looked straight at Elymas and said, 'You are a child of the devil and an enemy of everything that is right! You are full of all kinds of deceit and trickery. Will you never stop perverting the right ways of the Lord?'" (vv. 9–10).

For the Christian, divine boldness comes from communion with and the filling of God the Holy Spirit. That's how the apostle Paul—a man gripped with the fear of death—could speak so boldly in the face of persecution and resistance. That's how he could be stoned, left for dead, and drag his

DIVINE BOLDNESS
*comes from communion with and
the filling of God the Holy Spirit.*

broken body back into the very place of his persecution to continue preaching the gospel of our Lord on the next day (Acts 14:19–20). He was filled with God the Holy Spirit, who gives boldness and power to witness. He didn't flip a switch; God took over. This is what we need in our efforts to share the gospel with our friends and neighbors: we need God the Holy Spirit to take over.

A FUNNY THING HAPPENED DURING OUR DIALOGUE

We arrived that night at the venue for the dialogue. I was afraid, but tried to project calm and warmth. Before the event began, I asked the young man traveling with me to find a relatively safe distance from which to watch the event.

The discussion began and a funny thing happened. Someone seemed to take over. For nearly three hours, the Muslim speaker and I presented our sides. We questioned each other. We engaged with the audience. It was great!

It wasn't me! I was still afraid, and I hadn't shared any details about my conversion from Islam to faith in the Lord Jesus. Quietly, I carried on another debate with myself. *Should I? Should I not?* Was this fear or wisdom?

Finally, the moderator instructed my opponent and me to begin our closing comments. The other speaker mostly used his time to respond to a number of points raised earlier in the debate. In his closing minute, he then exhorted the audience to read the Quran for themselves. He insisted that if they would just read the Quran, it would improve their lives.

As I listened, it was as though I felt a tap on my shoulder, a nudge really. It was the Lord. When my fellow speaker closed by saying, "Read the Quran, it will improve your life," I knew the Lord was holding open the door for the gospel and my own testimony of conversion.

I took my turn at the rostrum, extended a few "thank-you's" to the organizers, and began, "You know, I've read the Quran. I used to be a practicing Muslim . . ."

After the dialogue, there was a lot of warm interaction between everyone in attendance. Not the slightest glitch had occurred. A high-level government official even suggested we hold an event annually—bigger next time! My fears had lied to me. The Lord was in control.

On the ride home, my friend and host asked, "How did you feel about the discussion?" I let out a long sigh, looked through the sunroof of his SUV, and said, "I was scared to death." He was astonished. "Brother, you couldn't tell it. You were so bold in defending and proclaiming the cross."

Praise be to God who gives His people power to witness through His Holy Spirit! Our sharing the gospel with Muslims is no different from Paul sharing the crucifixion and resurrection with Jews of his day. In fact, there is a lot of similarity. And what Paul needed to boldly declare the truth, we need as well—the filling of the Holy Spirit. We need to be filled with the Spirit so desperately that God commands it in Ephesians 5:18.

When is the last time you prayed or asked others to pray for your boldness? In what situations in your life do you need boldness in the face of fear?

Remember God's command: Be filled with the Spirit.

Things *to* Remember

1. You don't have to be a super-apostle to share the gospel with Muslims. Even the apostle Paul faced fear and felt his weakness.

2. By the Holy Spirit we have power and boldness to witness for Christ in any situation. The Spirit who dwells in us will not leave us nor forsake us. He will give us what we need to testify of Christ.

Trust the Bible

I *cannot think* of one conversation with a Muslim friend where the reliability and authority of the Bible were not in question. In every spiritual conversation I can recall, my Muslim friend assumed the trustworthiness of the Quran and rejected in various ways the integrity of the Bible.

I don't blame my Muslim friends for taking this posture. The Quran's miraculous transmission is, after all, central to their faith. Without assuming it and defending it, they would be lost at sea.

But the same is true of Christians. Without assuming and defending the reliability of the Bible, its divinely inspired nature and its authority in faith and life, we would be without an anchor and adrift in a sea of relativism. So defending the Scriptures—at least assuming their reliability and truthfulness—becomes essential to effective witnessing conversations with our Muslim neighbors.

It doesn't take advanced degrees in Hebrew and Greek to use the Bible (though those are wonderful). All a Christian needs to present the gospel is trust in the Scripture and a willingness to demonstrate that trust by assuming their reliability.[1]

DIVINE APPOINTMENTS

In the summer of 2006, my family and I accepted the call to pastor First Baptist Church in Grand Cayman, Cayman Islands. I know, I know . . . "suffering for Jesus" in such a difficult place to serve Him. I wish I had a dollar for every time I've heard that.

And the truth is the most difficult part of coming to serve the wonderful people of First Baptist was the trip here. We were able to ship most of our belongings directly from Washington, D.C. However, our car needed to be shipped from Miami, which meant a long drive from D.C. with two young children, a wife five months pregnant, and a humid, late July stop at Disney World. I kept telling myself, *It will be fun. It will be fun. It will be fun.*

We stopped in North Carolina to visit with family and friends. While in Raleigh, my wife and I became ill with flu-like symptoms, so we visited an outpatient clinic for a check-up and maybe a prescription. We were directed to a patient room and asked to wait while our nurse finished up with another patient. At the time, I was reading Chawkat Moucarry's book, *The Prophet and the Messiah: An Arab Christian's Perspective on Islam and Christianity.*

Our nurse, Jamal, entered the room a few minutes after I settled back into my book. He was pleasant, but you could

tell the afternoon had been filled with rushing and frustration. Jamal spoke with the cadence and emphasis of a Middle
Easterner, and indeed he was. He greeted us and asked what
I was reading. I gave him the book's title and a two-sentence
summary.

"Oh, really," he replied. "Are you a student of comparative religion?"

I thought to myself, *If I had a dollar for every time a Muslim
apologist began with that question. . .* Not yet sensing a divine
appointment, I offered a nasally and lukewarm, "Yes."

Jamal followed up. "Why?"

"Well, in part because I'm a pastor," I said. And before I
could elaborate or offer a more compelling answer than "I'm
a pastor," my new Muslim friend took the floor. He vented a
little about American foreign policy, media depiction of Muslims, religious liberty (strangely he thought Saudi Arabia a
freer place religiously than the United States), and occasion-
ally compared Christianity and Islam.

I nodded here and there (inside kicking myself for the
many rebuttals I missed or weak spots I couldn't exploit).
Periodically I tried to ask a question to keep the discussion
focused on the central issue: Jesus. He was happy as a
Muslim apologist to offer his thoughts about the Lord.

BIBLE CONTRADICTIONS?

Pretty soon Jamal launched into a bit of his own personal
story, how he came to believe fervently in Islam. His family
migrated to the United States from Jordan; he served in the
military; and as an adult studying comparative religion

became convinced that Islam was the absolute truth. He asked me if I believed in truth.

"Sure," I replied.

Then out came his ace. "You know, the Bible is full of all kinds of contradictions. Thousands of them. So it can't be true."

I smiled and asked, "Can you name one?"

My friend replied, "Trust me. There are many. I can't name one off the top of my head, but I have a list at home and I will share it with you."

I explained that the Quran didn't teach that there were contradictions and errors in the Bible but that, in fact, the Torah, Gospels, and Psalms of David are revelations from God. I referred to the three passages that teach that the message of the Torah was obscured or concealed by Jews during Muhammad's day and the one passage that accuses Christians of "forgetting" the message of the Gospels, but that nowhere in the Quran does it state that the revelation was changed.

I pressed a bit further and told my new friend that if he were to accept the Quran's teaching, he would eventually have to reject Islam because the Quran affirms the Bible and the authentic prophethood of Jesus. And the Bible reveals that Jesus is God the Son who died and rose again for the sins of the world and that everyone must repent of their sins and believe in Him for eternal life.

JAMAL'S CHALLENGE

My new friend paused before offering his conclusion. "If you can convince me that what you say is true—and I'm not one of those people who say mockingly, 'Prove God to me'—then I will convert. I will become a Christian. But no one leaves Islam because it is the truth. Show me one person who converted from Islam and I will convert."

Okay, you can call me a bit slow on recognizing appointments from God. But it was not until this point that I thought, *Oh! This is a divine appointment. God is up to something here.*

As Jamal put his hand on the door to leave the examination room, I asked if he was serious about wanting to know the truth and about converting if he found one person who converted from Islam and could answer his questions. He assured me he was. So I said, "You know, you're looking at a man who was once a Muslim and has converted to Christianity."

HE LOOKED AT ME
like he'd found some curious creature from a science fiction movie.

For the first time Jamal fell silent. He looked at me like he'd found some curious creature from a science fiction movie. "Really?" he asked.

"Really," I replied.

With what looked like genuine curiosity, he asked, "Why?"

"Because of all of the contradictions in Islam and the truth that is found in Jesus Christ."

He reflected on that for a few seconds. We spent the next few minutes putting our schedules together to find some time to talk further about Christianity and Islam. Before we left, he asked, "Why would you want to get together with me if you're a pastor? You're probably not going to change your mind, so why meet with me?"

"Because," I responded, "I would like nothing more than to see you come to faith in Jesus Christ and become a Christian."

The nine-hundred-mile drive from Washington, D.C., to Miami began with a not-so-enthusiastic husband. But just a few hours drive from D.C., the Lord made it clear that He had other purposes for the drive. One of which was to meet Jamal so that he might see a Christian simply express confidence in the Bible.

We didn't engage in a long game of Bible ping-pong or a Quranic version of Trivial Pursuit. We simply began as two men putting their trust in the reliability of their sacred texts—Jamal in the Quran, me in the Bible. And the Lord used that to open an opportunity for the gospel.

MUSLIM OBJECTIONS TO THE BIBLE: "THE BIBLE HAS CONTRADICTIONS"

Some Muslims use a number of objections to the reliability of the Scriptures in an attempt to weaken Christian confidence in the Bible. None of the objections offer satisfying or compelling critiques of the Bible, and often our Muslim friends are simply repeating what they have heard or read from Muslim leaders and literature. After a few evangelistic conversations, most people will identify a few recurring criticisms of the Bible.

The first is, "The Bible has contradictions." Jamal relied heavily on perhaps the most popular but misinformed criticism: supposed contradictions. Even people of no religious faith will sometimes dismiss the Bible because they heard or read somewhere that it is "full of contradictions."

But you've read the Bible. Have you seen any contradictions? Certainly there are difficult things to interpret in the Bible. And there are varying interpretations of difficult texts by godly, well-meaning Christians. Rival interpretations exist in every religion and philosophical school of thought. But rival interpretations are not the same as contradictions, where a statement is both asserted and denied at the same time. A contradiction would say something such as: "Jesus said He is God." And then follow with: "Jesus said He is not God but came to honor God." Both statements cannot be true.

The Bible has no contradictions in it. The Lord God does not contradict Himself. So we can express confidence in the Bible by simply asking those who make such a charge to put forth the evidence. Jamal couldn't produce one contradiction from Scripture—not because he wasn't skilled enough but because there is none in the Bible.

MUSLIM OBJECTIONS TO THE BIBLE: "THE BIBLE HAS BEEN CHANGED"

Jamal also held the popular view that the Bible had been corrupted or changed over the years. He believed that the followers of Christ over the centuries had removed things that pointed to the coming of Muhammad and the truth of the Quran. Again, there is no evidence for this. Moreover, the responsibility lies with those who make the charge to make their case, especially since neither the Quran nor the Hadith clearly allege corruption or change of the Scripture but rather misunderstanding of the Scripture. If the Bible had been corrupted, why would the Quran have confirmed it nearly six hundred years later?[2]

The Bible is the best attested ancient manuscript in history. With the thousands of manuscripts and fragments, along with quotations from early church fathers existing in multiple languages and cultures, we may have complete confidence that the writings of the Old and New Testament are reliably transmitted from those who first received and believed its message from God.

MORE OBJECTIONS TO THE BIBLE: "JESUS NEVER SAID THAT!"

Often, Muslims will insist that Christians use only the parts of the Bible recording the words of our Lord. They argue that the writers of Scripture misinterpret the teachings of God, so they want to limit discussions to only certain portions. Often along with this attitude toward Scripture comes the insistence that the exact words be in the text itself. So, once a Muslim man demanded that I show him where Jesus said "I am God" in those exact words. I suppose we might call these persons "red letter Muslims."

But Christians should not accept this premise any more than a Muslim should be made to discard the Quran. Muslims believe that companions of the prophet faithfully transmitted Muhammad's teachings to print, and they trust that transmission. Likewise, we owe no explanation for trusting that under the Spirit of God prophets and apostles recorded the teachings of Christ and teachings about Christ as God intended (see 2 Timothy 3:16–17; 2 Peter 1:20–21). The words in red are not more or less inspired than the words in black type. The writers of the words in red were the same writers of the words in black. All of God's Word is reliable and shall stand until all is fulfilled (Matthew 5:18). We may safely trust that what Paul or Matthew or John wrote is the divinely inspired Word of God.

CONTEXT, CONTEXT, CONTEXT

After a couple of phone calls, Jamal and I were finally able to set a lunch date. He proved eager to meet and discuss things further. We selected a quiet restaurant and met after midday prayer.

Our lunch meeting was an exciting time. I planned to start by sharing my own conversion testimony with him, with a slow explication of the gospel included. When I sat down, Jamal said, "So . . . tell me about your life from A to Z." Open door.

I offered my testimony of conversion and began to briefly "unpack" the gospel. Then Jamal wanted to discuss the reliability of the Quran and the Bible. A couple days prior, Jamal confidently had asserted that the Bible had thousands of errors and contradictions but could not cite one. Now he produced an Islamic study center document outlining supposed contradictions, with verses and parts of verses taken out of context and read with a wooden literalism.

So we opened the Bible to each of the passages, read several verses before and after the disputed verses, discussed their meaning, and tried to lift up the gospel implications of

the texts. It was a short course in how to read the Scriptures—nothing fancy, really. Nearly every criticism Jamal
had of a passage of Scripture was answered right there in the
immediate context of the passage!

And while we studied, I reminded Jamal of the several
passages from the Quran that described the Torah, Gospels,
and Psalms of David as revelation from God.[3] My question
was: "If, as you believe, the Bible was corrupted by the time
of the Quran's writing (six hundred years after Christ and
the apostles), why does the Quran confirm the Bible?"

Jamal evaded the question with hypothetical scenarios
and dogmatic assertions. I wasn't able to help Jamal accept
the entire Bible as God's revelation. But by God's grace, he
did stop insisting that I not look to all of the Scripture as
solid ground for my belief. From that point, we more or less
continued the discussion as though the Bible were true and
reliable, which allowed the work of evangelism to continue
more directly. With little more than reading a few passages
in their context, the Lord allowed me to move on with pre-
senting the good news to Jamal.

IF WE TRUST IT, LET'S USE IT

There is one final way Christians can demonstrate their
trust in the Bible in Muslim evangelism. By opening and
using the Bible, we demonstrate our reliance on the Scripture
as the Word of God and our dependence on its message rather
than human wisdom. Sometimes the best defense is a good
offense. When we make our case from the Scripture, we
implicitly signal its trustworthiness and authority.

Sometimes Christians fear that defending the Scriptures will offend their Muslim and other non-Christian acquaintances. But in my experience, Muslims respect Christians more deeply when we stand firm in our belief in the Scripture as the Word of God. They like to think of themselves as having an unwavering faith in the Quran. So a supposedly faithful Christian who does not honor the sacred Scriptures appears weak and untrustworthy to many Muslims. We gain ground in our evangelism simply by refusing to be embarrassed about the Scriptures and trusting that the Bible is the Word of God.

Things *to* Remember

1. The Bible is a trustworthy book. Most of the Muslim objections to the Bible may be answered simply by reading things in their context. Always read a few verses before and following the "disputed" verse or verses to be sure things are being read in context.

2. Use the Bible in your evangelism. Using the Scripture demonstrates your trust in it.

Be Hospitable

"How do you find our hospitality?"

That was the first question my young Middle Eastern friend asked me immediately following our introduction. I'd been in the United Arab Emirates for about two days, and he wanted to know how the people famed for their hospitality were doing. Rather rotund with a puffy dark beard, his face registered a mixture of pride regarding Arab hospitality and determination to do something if for some reason I had not found myself well-treated.

My immediate impression was, *Wow. I've never been asked that before. I wonder how many Christians ever ask that question of strangers they meet? Is hospitality an all but lost practice in the Christian faith?*

Now, I could do certain mental gymnastics to disregard the kindness I received by saying something such as, "None of this counts because they're not in Christ." But that would miss the point, I think. I *do* know Christ, and yet I'm afraid that I and perhaps many other Christians are not nearly as hospitable as this young man. Instead of trying to explain this away, it's better to repent than to reflect.

My questioner asked me that question several years ago now. I still ponder it from time to time. Whether it's from my proud, competitive, sinful heart, or some genuine conviction, I want to be more hospitable. I need to be more hospitable.

OUCH, THAT HURTS!

I know many Christians who have been hurt by other Christians, members of churches who have failed to love in one way or another. In God's grace, I've not had many incidents where I've suffered hurt at the hands of other Christians. But one of the more painful and confusing times in my Christian life involved the offer and repeated rejection of hospitality.

My wife and I had taken an interest in a new couple at the local church where we were members. The couple seemed to be full of joy and eagerness even though they were having a difficult time settling into the church community. As one of the few white families at a predominantly African American church, they no doubt had their challenges and could feel the cultural differences. So my wife and I reached out. We invited them to dinner on various weeknights, sought their fellowship on weekends and after church, and offered to host a dessert fellowship with a few other people from church with whom they might connect.

They declined each of our invitations. Lame excuse followed lame excuse, and in time we were hurt.

In retrospect, perhaps the couple was unaccustomed to such overtures. But that encounter and our little hurt taught us a lesson: It is painful to not be included in the lives of others, whether you're the one extending or hoping to receive hospitality.

WHAT KEEPS US FROM
SHOWING HOSPITALITY?

I don't know if the practice of hospitality is lost; perhaps that's an overstatement. But it does need some resuscitation, to be freshly modeled and taught. Even when they would really like to do so, many people find themselves hesitant to extend hospitality to others. Four factors contribute to the decline among Christians of hosting and acting generously toward others.

Privatization. It seems that some people feel burdened, inconvenienced, or uninterested in sharing their lives. A hardness of heart reflects itself in an unwillingness to open up to others, to invite them to our tables, and to serve them from the bounty the Lord has given us. Perhaps past hurts create a guardedness, or selfishness erodes the desire to share. But in any case, many people think of Christian living in exclusively private terms. They have reduced the faith to "a personal relationship with Jesus" without recognizing either our union with other Christians or the necessity of sharing the faith and their lives with non-Christians. When that happens, hospitality suffers.

Fear of man. For some people the fear of man plays a part

in undermining a culture of hospitality. That fear may take
the form of a fear of rejection. My wife and I could have
easily given in to that fear when our fellow members refused
our offers of hospitality. Or the fear of man may express itself
in embarrassment or shame at the prospect of having someone in their "meager" homes. A worldly mentality assumes
that to show hospitality we must have showcase homes and
fine place settings (at least as fine as that neighbor or friend
who has all the "really nice" stuff we covet). And so, some
Christians neglect this important ministry because they're
actually thinking of themselves and comparing themselves
to the wrong standard—other fallen men.

Passivity. Passivity is a third factor contributing to the
decline in hospitality. We can be too nonchalant in cultivating meaningful affection for one another. We wait for the
relationship to come to us. We want it to be "natural" and to
"just flow" or "click." There is such a thing as trying too hard,
but I think many of us are far from that. We try too little.
We'd rather enjoy the coziness of being alone with our own
thoughts, interests, and friends from some yesteryear like
high school or college. We don't like the toil of getting to
know others and opening ourselves up (much less "prying"
into their lives) in a substantive, transparent way. But for hospitality to thrive, we must relinquish our passive approach
to friendships.

Xenophobia. Some people fear others who are different
from themselves. They notice differences in appearance or
culture and they react with fear and distrust. Crossing cultural and ethnic boundaries seems as impossible and dangerous as Evil Knievel jumping the Grand Canyon in a

homemade rocket motorcycle. Consequently, Muslims in our neighborhood are ostracized rather than embraced, avoided rather than entertained. Hospitality is set aside in favor of fear.

WHY PRACTICE HOSPITALITY?

Muslims, who typically practice hospitality on a regular basis, value such actions by others. When we show hospitality, we welcome them into our lives. But even more important than showing hospitality to win friends and provide a platform for sharing our values and faith, we should practice hospitality for a number of biblical and practical reasons. Let me list four major reasons for overcoming our weaknesses and fears to practice hospitality toward Muslims.

First, the Bible commands Christians to be hospitable. "Share with God's people who are in need. Practice hospitality" (Romans 12:13). We practice hospitality because our sovereign God requires it of us. Our obedience to His command shows He is lord of our lives (Luke 6:46) and that we love Him (John 14:15, 20). Because the practice of hospitality is an act of joyful and loving obedience, we "offer hospitality to one another without grumbling" (1 Peter 4:9).

Second, hospitality allows us to care for the strangers among us, treating them fairly and kindly. God's Word shows special concern for strangers. Because the Lord's people have at times been strangers in foreign lands, they are to show compassion to the aliens within their gates (Exodus 22:21; 23:9). For many first-generation Muslims in the United States, there is a sense of alienation and uncertainty that American

Christians can lighten by inviting them into homes for meals and fun activities.

Third, the Bible teaches that our caring for strangers in a certain sense renders service to Jesus Himself (Matthew 25:34–40). Acts of mercy performed for the "least" of people among us are acts rendered ultimately to God Himself who cares for the widow, the orphan, and the stranger. What more practical way to make love for the lost more tangible than to open our homes and our calendars in a way that invites intimacy and friendship?

Fourth, hospitality is one mark of Christian maturity and godliness. That is why the Lord requires church leaders (1 Timothy 3:2) and widows receiving church assistance (1 Timothy 5:10) to be hospitable. Every Christian should aspire to serve in this way, just as our Lord came not to be served but to serve.

A PRACTICAL AND STRATEGIC OPPORTUNITY

The biblical commands to serve others also position us to take practical advantage of unique opportunities. Maybe the best way for us Christians to build friendships with Muslim neighbors the Lord has brought to our doorsteps is to host them in our homes. We may reach the world for Christ by simply reaching across our picket fences or crossing the street and then inviting them into our dining and family rooms.

Most Muslim growth, in places like the United States, starts with a small trickle of immigration. Followers of Islam enter America as "strangers," often without family or friends. They come as international students or as workers seeking opportunity. When they first arrive and when they have few others to lean on, Christians have a strategic opportunity to extend a welcoming hand of hospitality and to speak with them of the gospel. Yet the overwhelming majority of internationals in places like the United States never enter an American home.

Ridwan and I became friends while working on a project in Washington, D.C. Although almost twenty years separated us in age, we enjoyed one another's company. Ridwan, the older one, had fled Iran with his family during Ayatollah Khomeini's rise to power in 1979. After a few stops in various places, they immigrated to the United States. Life in the United States bewildered the entire family, especially his parents who felt the dizzying pace of American life and uneasiness with many American cultural patterns. They faced many difficulties, being suspected by most Americans who knew anything about their ethnic and religious backgrounds, and not always finding acceptance with Muslims holding differing political views. Ridwan recalled how they felt like strangers in a strange land with no one to befriend or guide them.

Many Muslims continue to feel this way until they find community with other Muslims. Often Christians remain distant when they notice the stranger; later they complain when the Muslim community becomes seemingly impenetrable to us. Let's welcome the stranger from the start. We can invite them into our homes and into the events of our lives. Let's prayerfully work to place ourselves inside those communities as they form and grow. If there was ever a time to "get in on the ground floor," this is it.

To witness to Muslims, we must place ourselves in the way of Muslim neighbors and friends. We can do that by waiting in alleys and pouncing on them with tracts and loud shouts when they pass by. (Please don't do that!) Or we can use what the Lord has given us in the way of living rooms, kitchen tables, food and drink, community outings, and family celebrations to invite a Muslim friend to experience Christian hospitality. Along the way, they can "taste and see that the Lord [Jesus] is good" (Psalm 34:8).

As one author put it: "It's not out of obligation that we should reach out to Muslims but in friendship. We have the right and the power afforded to us by Jesus Christ to be the most benevolent and generous people in the world, who seek not our own happiness but place our happiness in doing good to others."[1]

CHRISTIAN HOSPITALITY IN ACTION

Those who practice hospitality, from the most simple to the most generous gestures, find that the Lord often uses these overtures to produce spiritual fruit. A number of examples come to mind.

Kendria is a dear friend who works in an English as a second language (ESL) program in a major city. She befriended a Muslim supervisor at work, patiently listening to his criticisms of Christianity and Christians. After hearing his opinions for some time, one day she became impatient and "let him have it." Almost immediately afterward, she felt God convicting her for her sin against her coworker. So, one morning she made her way to his office and apologized for her sin against him. Her coworker was shocked that she would apologize. They had a pleasant conversation, at the end of which she worked up the nerve to invite this male coworker to church. To her surprise, he agreed to come.

Kendria very faithfully showed her friend around the church, guided him through the service for the morning, and introduced him to a number of friends. Her humility and hospitality, and the church's kindness, provided a brilliant testimony that refuted some of this man's perspectives about Christians.

Karen works with international students now living in the United States. At one prayer meeting at her church, she shared that the overwhelming majority of international students never enter an American home during their time in the United States. One campus student initiative estimates that 80 percent of international students never interact meaningfully with Americans.

But Karen wisely and graciously combines her work in English as a second language with Christian hospitality. She organizes ESL activities at her church, involves members of the church as tutors and hosts for the international students, and organizes occasional outings and gatherings where international students and Christians can interact. Once she invited a number of students to attend a Christian wedding, and exposed them to Christian hospitality and relationships in the wedding reception that followed. Friendship and gospel opportunity blossomed out of her thoughtfulness.

Stephanie, a medical student from a Hindu background, turned to the Lord in faith during a Communion service at her local church. Filled with joy in Christ, she shared her hope and love for Christ with her Muslim roommate. Eventually, she invited her roommate to attend church with her. Many of her brothers and sisters in Christ were surprised to see a young Muslim woman dressed in traditional coverings attend church that Sunday morning. But they responded with eager kindness and hospitality, helping Stephanie to further her relationship with her roommate.

A couple years ago I was invited to speak at the Bangor Worldwide Missions Convention in Northern Ireland. While we were there, my wife and I received some of the warmest hospitality and offers of friendship we had ever known. The saints of Northern Ireland were not only kind to us, but their hospitality expressed itself in gospel concern for Muslim people. One night during the convention, an elderly lady approached me with a slightly nervous and out of place young man in tow. She had invited the Muslin friend to this event, and now introduced herself and her friend. With graciousness and love, she shared with me some details of her own life and faith, and then she prompted conversation with the young Muslim man.

CHRISTIANS MUST
be ready to house and care for new believers from Muslim backgrounds.

Before our ten minutes were over, the Lord had placed two new friends in my life and hopefully planted seeds for future gospel conversation with our Muslim friend. Her simple hospitality shown in inviting this young man—living in a foreign country with no real spiritual friendships—may result in eternal life. I pray so.

Though many of the examples above do not mention spectacular conversions, conversions do happen. And when they do, our hospitality work has not ended—it's just beginning in many cases. Because some Muslims come from families that will disown them for faith in Christ, Christians must be ready to house and care for new believers from Muslim backgrounds.

John pastors a local church in a predominantly Muslim country. The length and depth of John's hospitality was tested when one young woman repented of her sins and trusted in the work of Jesus as her substitute and Savior. After experiencing God's grace in Christ, her family treated her as if she were dead. John and his family took in this new believer and welcomed her as part of their own family. John's home became her home, and the church family became her family. Through their love and care, Christ gave this young woman brothers and sisters, fathers and mothers one hundred times those she had lost for His sake.

WOMEN REACHING WOMEN
For Women Only: Hospitality to Muslim Women

American women have an opportunity that American men can never have when it comes to hospitality. Most Muslim women will have meaningful social contact only with other women and the men of their families. Great effort is made to protect the modesty and safety of Muslim women by keeping them secluded from men in general.

Conversations from men would be unwanted and ineffective. Yet, the opportunities for Christian women may be plentiful. If you're a Christian woman, I encourage you to recognize the unique role you can play in reaching out to Muslim women. It begins with developing friendships and showing hospitality.

Many Muslim women will know very few people outside their own families, so establishing relationships can be slow and difficult. I know two godly wives and mothers who labor with their husbands in the Middle East. Leanne and Keri share their husbands' visions for seeing Muslim people come to know the love and grace of God through Jesus Christ. They are faithful members of their local churches. And they are committed to their unique role in sharing the gospel with Muslim women.

In the United States, women face the same challenge—it takes time to develop friendships and a trusting, open relationship. But humanly speaking, the primary access Muslim women in America will have to the gospel may just be the Christian women who graciously befriend them. And such friendships typically include hospitality.

This chapter points out the importance of being hospitable. Hospitality creates opportunity. In many cases, inviting a Muslim woman over for tea and conversation provides a safe opportunity to talk and to get to know one another. Ideally, this might be done one-on-one, when men are away from the home. Women who work inside the home may have the most flexibility for this aspect of ministry to Muslim women.

Shirin Taber offers some wonderful advice when it comes to hosting Muslim women in your home. "When it's your turn to invite Shandiz and Mitra to your home, make the first impression count. Your coffee table should have an abundance of pastries or party foods, such as cookies, nuts, fruit, and chips. Offer your guests several cups of tea or coffee, insisting they have another, since it is the Muslim custom to politely refuse the first offer or refill. Always serve your guest first (a platter of cookies or seconds at the dinner table) before serving yourself. Lavish them with love. Make them feel like a king or queen."[2]

Knowing Muslim customs shows you are sensitive and thoughtful of the other person. Just as Westerners struggle with stereotypes of Muslim women, Muslim men and women struggle with stereotypes of Western women. Many Muslims are uncomfortable with Western standards of dress. I've sometimes been embarrassed to see scantily clad Western men or women in predominantly Muslim contexts where modesty entails wearing complete coverings. And to be honest, immodesty is a problem even for many Christian women.

Ladies, as you reach out to female Muslim acquaintances and their families, be sure to dress modestly and tastefully. Wear things you might wear to church or to a somewhat formal gathering. Your modesty will commend the gospel (1 Peter 3:4–5) and help others to feel comfortable with you.

Moreover, be sure the children dress modestly. Muslims believe children are a reflection of their parents. The children's immodesty will discredit their parents. Young girls should especially be careful to clad themselves in ways that communicate respect for themselves and others, avoiding provocative attire altogether. Shorts and sleeveless shirts as well as tattered jeans can distract, even dismay your Muslim guests.

In time, the Lord may allow you to introduce your Muslim friend to a wider circle of Christian women. Do so as your friend gives you opportunity and shows comfort. During college, Stephanie shared an apartment with Sharifa, a young Muslim woman. Their close living arrangement provided many moments of intimacy and relationship-building. As Stephanie lived out her faith, Sharifa grew more comfortable with both Stephanie and her Christian friends. Eventually, Sharifa felt safe enough with Stephanie and her friends to attend church where she heard the gospel preached clearly.

ARE YOU HOSPITABLE?

God makes clear in Scripture His command to show hospitality. Our generosity provides opportunities to live out the gospel in practical and meaningful ways. In Christ, God brought those who were far off near to Him (Ephesians 2:13) and made alienated enemies His own children (Romans 5:6–10). When we open our lives and homes to others among us, we imitate the kindness and love of God (Ephesians 5:1).

Do you show hospitality to others? Are you helpful to those in need? Is your home open to the "strangers" and "aliens" in your neighborhood? Who has God put in your path so that the love of Christ might be seen in your warm welcome and care? All around us are opportunities to make Christ known to our Muslim friends. Are you ready to seize those opportunities for the Lord?

Things *to* Remember

1. God commands His people to be hospitable. By being hospitable, the Lord opens numerous opportunities for friendships and evangelism.

2. Most immigrants to the United States never enter an American home or a Christian home. Serving strangers and those who are in need is one way we serve our Lord.

Use Your
Local Church

The Muslim-Christian dialogue ended with great energy. Much had been said and the audience still had questions and comments.

We faced a battery of questions during the formal question-and-answer session before the discussion ended. As the audience began to leave, some members came to the front to talk more. Though the question had been asked earlier in the Q&A portion of the program, Farhud asked it again: "Why are Christians so immoral?"

In his experience, Christians lived in ways that no Muslim would respect as honoring to God. "Why did Christians drink, smoke, have sex outside of marriage, and a host of other things?" he asked.

Surrounded by a small huddle of questioners, I could tell that Farhud was not the only one with this concern.

Heads nodded in agreement as people leaned in to hear the answer.

IS THE CHURCH FULL OF HYPOCRITES?

To be honest, there was a time where I felt the same way Farhud felt. As far as I could tell, the Christians I knew were all hypocrites, preaching a high standard of morality and living well beneath it, imposing on others their values but not caring to observe those values themselves. I used to think that Christians were all living versions of Paul Laurence Dunbar's classic poem, "We Wear the Mask":

> We wear the mask that grins and lies,
> It hides our cheeks and shades our eyes,—
> This debt we pay to human guile;
> With torn and bleeding hearts we smile,
> And mouth with myriad subtleties.
>
> Why should the world be over-wise,
> In counting all our tears and sighs?
> Nay, let them only see us, while
>   We wear the mask.
>
> We smile, but, O great Christ, our cries
> To thee from tortured souls arise.
> We sing, but oh the clay is vile
> Beneath our feet, and long the mile;
> But let the world dream otherwise,
>   We wear the mask![1]

Dunbar's poem, first published in 1896, originally described the strategy of many African Americans coping with the anguish of life in a segregated America. Outwardly they donned a smiling mask, but inwardly cries arose from "tortured souls." That seemed a pretty good description of church people to me. Before I became a Christian, I suspected that churches were full of hypocrites.

Then I became a Christian and I knew that Farhud and I were correct: Churches are full of hypocrites. But I discovered four things that I didn't know before.

First, most of the Christians inside the churches mourned over their own shortcomings. Their "hypocrisy" often reflected their weakness, not wickedness. They fought against their flesh and their sin, longing to be conformed to Christ. I could see the weaknesses before, but now I could see the heart as well. I had not known from the outside what spiritual striving existed inside the church. And that striving far surpassed any resistance to sin that I had seen outside the church.

> AVOIDING HYPOCRISY
> *is not a matter of morality
> but primarily a matter of
> supernatural renewal that
> produces the born again life.*

Second, I learned that the "hypocrisy" of Christians was far less dangerous than the hypocrisy of non-Christians. Whatever weakness corrupts the testimony of Christians, that weakness is benign compared to the intentional deceit and scheming of people who love their sin and are enslaved to it. The vindictive hypocrisy of those outside the church injures, maims, and kills far more efficiently, effectively, and thoroughly than any hypocrisy resident in Christian churches.

Third, I learned that Christians fight against hypocrisy because they love their Savior who died for their hypocrisy. The gospel speaks to hypocrisy in a way that Islam and secular philosophies never could. Christ died for hypocrites and by His grace transforms them into sons of righteousness. Avoiding hypocrisy is not a matter of morality and rule-keeping, but primarily a matter of supernatural renewal that produces the born-again life. What seemed like superficial, make-believe happiness masking deep despair and unrighteousness was genuine joy at having been forgiven for all their transgressions. Christians were not wearing masks so much as delighting in the victory and freedom found in Jesus' forgiveness.

Finally, it became clear to me that Farhud and I mistook Christians for Westerners. Much of the Muslim concern about how "Christians" behave comes from equating Christianity with Western culture generally. Most Muslims don't realize that Christians agonize over Hollywood films, immodesty, promiscuity, drunkenness, violence, misogyny, out-of-control youth culture, and other social ills. Those things are not the Christian faith. Moreover, many professing Muslims living in lands with greater freedoms also participate in these ills. The church has her faults, but she should not be blamed for the sinful productions of a fallen culture any more than all Muslims should be blamed for the terrorist actions of a few.

The church is full of *former* hypocrites *redeemed* from their hypocrisy by the love of God in Christ Jesus. So, exposing our Muslim friends to the true church doesn't hinder but aids our efforts to make the gospel clear to them.

THE LOCAL CHURCH AND EVANGELISM

The local church functions like a gospel-spreading co-op. In fact, that seems to be what the apostle Paul had in mind when he praised God for the Philippian church, who shared or partnered with him in the gospel (Philippians 1:4–5). Even while Paul was in chains, the Philippian Christians continued the work of spreading the testimony about Jesus.

Likewise, when we are limited in some way in our evangelistic efforts, our brothers and sisters in Christ may be used by the Lord to advance His message to our Muslim friends. Such cooperative evangelism can speak the truth about Jesus' mission even when we find ourselves at a loss for words. We need words to communicate the gospel, but those words should be set like a diamond in the goal setting of the local church.

As she lives out the faith and life found in Christ, the local church testifies to the truth of the gospel in ways that individuals can't. Joshua Harris makes this clear when he writes:

One thing a local congregation does best is to show your non-Christian neighbors that the *new life* made available through Jesus' death on the cross is also the foundation for a *new society*. By living the gospel as a distinct community, the church down the street accomplishes the important mission of displaying the transforming effects of the gospel for the world to see.

Others won't be able to see this larger picture if we remain detached from each other and go our separate ways.[2]

Harris provides eloquent argument for both the necessity of membership in the local church and for the centrality of the local church in our evangelism. Far from something to be ashamed of or to criticize, the church displays the compelling beauty of the gospel like nothing else on earth. We see this in at least three ways.

LOVE WITHIN THE LOCAL CHURCH CLARIFIES WHAT TRUE DISCIPLESHIP LOOKS LIKE

Contemporary Christianity tends to view the work of evangelism in terms of a person's method of convincing others to "make a decision" to follow Christ. It's not my purpose here to complete a review of evangelistic methods employed by any particular individuals or organizations. But I do hope to point out something that has been lost in so much writing about and practice of evangelism: the local church.

It seems clear that Jesus intends the local church to be an aid, not a hindrance, to witnessing to others. In John 13:34–35, the Lord states: "A new command I give you: Love one another. As I have loved you, so you must love one another. *By this all men will know that you are my disciples, if you love one another*" (italics added).

Notice the Master intends that the love shared between Christian disciples be so radical and tangible that "all men" will be able to see that we are followers of Jesus. Love distinguishes genuine disciples of Christ from the "Christian culture" or the heritage of Western society. A community of love across ethnic, cultural, and age distinctions testifies powerfully to the truth of the gospel.

THE UNITY OF THE LOCAL CHURCH REVEALS THAT CHRIST HAS COME

In His high priestly prayer in John 17, our Lord prayed to the Father on behalf of all those who would believe in Him. One of the chief things Jesus prayed for on that day was the unity of His followers:

> My prayer is not for them alone. I pray also for those who will believe in me through their message, *that all of them may be one*, Father, just as you are in me and I am in you. May they also be in us so *that the world may believe that you have sent me*. I have given them the glory that you gave me, *that they may be one as we are one*: I in them and you in me. *May they be brought to complete unity to let the world know that you sent me and have loved them even as you have loved me.* (vv. 20–23, italics added)

Islam makes much of its claim to be a universal religion. Muslims boast of the many different peoples who practice the faith.

But here, Jesus prays not just for an outward universality but an abiding spiritual oneness. He prays that all of His followers should experience a unity like that that He shares with the Father. Jesus intends that Christian spiritual unity should communicate certain truths to the world. It should tell the world that the Father has sent the Son.

When we strive to maintain unity in the church (Ephesians 4:3), to practically live out the reality already accomplished by Christ on the cross (Ephesians 2:14–18), we send a powerful message to a watching world. We say, "Jesus has come from the Father. The Father loves His people just as He loves His Son." Muslims need to know that message, and they may see it in the unity of our local churches.

THE LOCAL CHURCH REVEALS THE WISDOM OF GOD

Even among many Christians, however, the church suffers a sullied reputation. Her weakness and imperfections receive the most attention, while her strengths and power lie unused. As Christians, we need to recover something of the splendor and majesty of the church, which consists of God's redeemed people.

With all of her problems, the church still brings praise and glory to God. The apostle Paul points out that the church actually reveals a mystery hidden in ages past—that Jew and Gentile should be fellow heirs and members of the same body. The apostle writes that "through the church, the manifold wisdom of God" is made known "to the rulers and authorities in the heavenly realms" (Ephesians 3:6, 9–10). The reason he preaches the gospel, he says, is to declare the "manifold"—diverse, variegated—wisdom of God known to the world through the church.

All kinds of wisdom from God go on display to all the

powers in the spiritual realm through the church. Do you know what angels and redeemed men and even demons—who oppose God's plan—must say when they look upon God's creation of the church? They cry out "Wisdom! Indisputable and glorious wisdom! God, You are so wise!"

Have you ever had the experience of children or grandchildren bringing you a picture they've drawn or a craft they've made at school? They arrive really proud of their creation. They call out, "Mom, Dad (Grandma, Grandpa), look at what I made!" The kind parent or grandparent looks at the picture, smiles, and places a gentle hand on the child's shoulders, saying, "This is a beautiful giraffe." The child looks at you slightly puzzled and says, "No, it's a picture of the family on vacation."

That's one of the priceless moments children give to us. When it happens, we pretend we recognize "the family." Not wishing to discourage the aspiring Rembrandt, we conclude, "That's a beautiful family portrait." Then we hang it on the refrigerator door. We basically humor the child and offer an encouragement because of the potential we hope to develop in them. We love them so we fudge the truth a little.

But when God hangs the church on the refrigerator door of the universe, no one humors God by saying, "Well, you've got potential." Everyone—everything—angels fallen and holy—look at God's creation of the church, His re-creation of sinners and rebels, and says, "Wow! What an indescribable display of wisdom!"

When we see the church, our reaction should be reverence and awe. He has made Himself our God and made us His people. Rather than critique and disparage, we should cry, "Oh my God," not in vain but in awe and wonder and love because only God could create such a beautiful display and only He has wisdom to do it.

SO USE YOUR LOCAL CHURCH

All of this means that membership and involvement in a local church makes the work of evangelism significantly easier. Displaying Christian love becomes easier when living out the faith with those not like you instead of trying to go it alone or in small clusters of people with the same background as yourself.

Likewise, Christian unity makes it easier to demonstrate that our claims about Jesus aren't individual idiosyncrasies. We follow Jesus not because we're odd people but because He is Lord of all, and our unity across natural boundaries reveals this.

How can we use our local church effectively in the effort to lovingly introduce our Muslim neighbors to Jesus Christ?

+ Invite your Muslim friends to join you at church services and other gatherings. Don't give in to the false stereotype that says Muslims will not be interested in coming to church. Some won't, but many will. Kindly invite them. Repeatedly invite them. Have confidence that the Lord will use His people to convey the truth about Jesus.
+ Start a prayer group with friends at church. Evangelism and conversion require our most fervent prayers. Regularly meeting with others to talk about

our witnessing opportunities and to ask the Lord's blessing provides the power needed to turn hearts and to make us bold in sharing.

✦ Pray for the preaching of the gospel in your local church. Your pastor needs the prayers of his people. Pray that the Bible would have a lasting impact on the person's own soul, and that the Lord would bless the preaching with power to save the lost.

✦ Organize social events with friends from church that include Muslim friends. Consider a Christmas tea where someone shares the gospel briefly and perhaps a word of encouragement. Organize an outing after a Sunday morning service. Invite non-Christians to the service and to the outing afterward. Be sure to discuss the service and answer questions that might be raised. Start an evangelistic Bible study specifically for Muslims, involving a couple of others from the church as well.

THE CHURCH ADORNS THE GOSPEL

The ways in which we can use our churches to adorn the gospel are legion. And we should use the corporate witness of the local church because God reveals so much about Himself and His Son through our local congregations. When Christians live together, using their spiritual gifts, God's grace is administered to His people (1 Peter 4:10). In all of our evangelistic efforts, we need fresh supplies of God's grace to enable us to persevere and to work zealously until He comes. That grace comes to us through the church.

The church is the pillar and foundation of the truth
(1 Timothy 3:15). From Sunday to Sunday, faithful pastors
lead their assemblies in celebrating the truth as Christians
sing, pray, and preach the Word of God. This makes the local
church an incredible ally in our efforts to spread the gospel
among Muslim people. As Charles Bridges once observed:

> The Church is the mirror that reflects the whole efful-
> gence of the Divine character. It is the grand scene, in
> which the perfections of Jehovah are displayed to the
> universe. The revelations made to the Church—the
> successive grand events in her history and, above all,
> the manifestation of "the glory of God in the Person of
> Jesus Christ"—furnish even to the heavenly intelli-
> gences fresh subjects of adoring contemplation.[3]

Things *to* Remember

1. The local church is God's plan for demonstrating His wisdom and love in a fallen world. Consequently, every Christian should be an active member of a local church.

2. The local church provides opportunities to partner with other Christians in making the gospel known to our Muslim friends. We don't have to do the work of evangelism alone.

10

Suffer

for the Name

Following the September 11, 2001, terrorist attacks on New York's World Trade Center and the Pentagon, a well-known Christian talk show host got himself into a bit of trouble for commending what he saw as a kind of courage in the terrorists responsible for the attacks. He commended their commitment in dying for the cause of Islam.

The talk show host's words were careless and injured a lot of people affected by those heinous acts. Yet what the commentator attempted to note is worth observing: Some Muslims appear willing to suffer great things for Islam. In contrast, many Christians seem unwilling to suffer for Christ.

THE POWER OF ISLAMIC JIHAD

Why do so many Muslims seem willing to suffer for the name of Allah? The key answer is the belief in *jihad*, which literally means to "strive" or "struggle." Usually, such striving by Muslims aims to accomplish one of two purposes: to advance individual piety (i.e., prayer, fasting, etc.) or to promote and defend Islam. Moderate Muslims tend to emphasize the spiritual aspects of jihad, while militants think of jihad in terms of armed struggle and conquest. In either case, the doctrine of jihad influences the practice of many Muslims. Many willingly sacrifice to promote Islam and to gain the rewards of paradise. For to struggle and die in the cause of Islam is the only thing that guarantees paradise for the Muslim.

One decade after the stunning attacks of 9/11, our TV sets still show with numbing regularity videos of bearded men wielding automatic weapons and al-Qaeda leader Osama bin Laden trekking across rugged Afghan hills. Historic footage of the Twin Towers smoking and collapsing conjure the memory of lives lost and sudden disaster. And the word *jihad* has become a regular part of American parlance synonymous with such images and attacks.

THE PLACE OF CHRISTIAN SUFFERING

While our televisions broadcast images of militaristic Islam and young jihadis preparing to kill and die for the cause, the same televisions broadcast Christian programs that feature preachers extolling the "blessings" of material prosperity, luxury, and ease. These programs define the Christian life not in terms of sacrifice, struggle, or the narrow way but in terms of wealth, possessions, and trouble-free living. As a consequence of such teaching on television—and in some churches—many have lost any sense that following Jesus will be costly. In addition, the material abundance in America makes many Christians comfortable with what they have and hesitant to suffer for the gospel.

As a result, Christian suffering goes homeless in the thinking of many.

However, references to the certainty of suffering for those who follow Jesus are plentiful in the New Testament:

If anyone would come after me, he must deny himself and take up his cross and follow me. For whoever wants to save his life will lose it, but whoever loses his life for me will find it. (Matthew 16:24–25)

In fact, everyone who wants to live a godly life in Christ Jesus will be persecuted. (2 Timothy 3:12)

For it has been granted to you on behalf of Christ not only to believe on him, but also to suffer for him. (Philippians 1:29)

But if you suffer for doing good and endure it, this is commendable before God. To this you were called, because Christ suffered for you, leaving you an example, that you should follow in his steps. (1 Peter 2:20b–21)

These references and many others devastate the "easy believism" and comfort-seeking of so much modern Christianity. From these passages, we may conclude that suffering is as central to the Christian life as faith. Indeed, we suffer because of our faith in Christ.

On the one hand, Christians are called to suffer for Christ. And yet, Christians do not respond to suffering or strive in the cause of Christ by resorting to violent and destructive means. Nothing could be more contrary to the work and character of Jesus our Savior! Jesus teaches us a radically different way to endure in the midst of suffering and to strive for His name. "You have heard that it was said, 'Love your neighbor and hate your enemy.' But I tell you: Love your enemies and pray for those who persecute you, that you may be sons of your Father in heaven" (Matthew 5:43–45a).

The apostles picked up Jesus' teaching and wrote to other Christians about them. Paul wrote to the Christians in Rome to remind them, "Do not repay anyone evil for evil. Be careful to do what is right in the eyes of everybody. If it is possible, as far as it depends on you, live at peace with everyone. Do not take revenge, my friends, but leave room for God's wrath, for it is written: 'It is mine to avenge; I will repay,' says the Lord" (Romans 12:17–19). Then Paul quotes Proverbs 25:21: "On the contrary: 'If your enemy is hungry, feed him; if he is thirsty, give him something to drink'" (v. 20a). James simply instructed, "Everyone should be quick to listen, slow to speak and slow to become angry, for man's anger does not bring about the righteous life that God desires" (James 1:19–20).

> WE ARE PROMISED
> *suffering, yet we deny the right to*
> *retaliation or counterattack.*

We are promised suffering, yet we deny the right to retaliation or counterattack. We endure hardship like good soldiers without resorting to violence.[1]

One of the most compelling examples of this Christian posture would be Dr. Martin Luther King Jr. and the nonviolent civil protests of the 1960s. African Americans suffered great violence for long centuries in American history. Inflicted pain did not discriminate between Christians and non-Christians. But not until Dr. King's prophetic call for African American Christians and all Americans to love their enemies and denounce violence would sufficient moral authority and spiritual power be gathered to overturn long-held patterns of affliction and suffering. The Christian ethic of loving your enemies and enduring suffering for righteousness sake ultimately proved socially and morally redemptive for an entire nation.

SUFFERING AS A CHRISTIAN . . .

No one looks forward to pain. We'd rather avoid it. And with good reason: Pain and suffering are unpleasant, discomforting, and wounding. Instinctively we look for ways around it. So how do we prepare for and endure suffering when it comes?

The Scripture doesn't just call us to times of suffering. Nor does it stop with limiting our responses in those times. Rather, the Scripture goes on to teach us how to endure when suffering comes. Remembering three things helps us in our affliction.

. . . BY REMEMBERING JESUS

Our Savior is the "Suffering Servant" of Isaiah 42 and 53. Jesus is acquainted with much sorrow and "has been tempted in every way, just as we are" (Hebrews 4:15). So, in our struggles, we are to remember that our Lord never reviled or rebuked when His tormenters attacked. Peter reminds his readers of how Jesus endured insult and threat as a pattern for their own endurance: "'He committed no sin, and no deceit was found in his mouth.' When they hurled their insults at him, he did not retaliate; when he suffered, he made no threats. Instead, he entrusted himself to him who judges justly" (1 Peter 2:22–23).

We are to call to mind our suffering Lord who faced trial with holiness and self-control. He is our pattern and example. As Ajith Fernando, director of a mission in war-torn Sri Lanka, put it, "The sight of our Savior loving us enough to die for us takes away the sting of unkind acts."[2] So, "we must glance at our problems and gaze at Jesus."[3]

. . . BY REMEMBERING GOD'S PROMISES

When Christians in the New Testament suffered for Christ, they recalled the promises of God to be a resource for both endurance and courage. The writer of Hebrews tells us of one such group of Christians who "stood [their] ground in a great contest in the face of suffering." Though at times they "were publicly exposed to insult and persecution at other times [they] stood side by side with those who were so treated," they "joyfully accepted the confiscation of [their] property," because they knew that they "had better and lasting possessions" (Hebrews 10:32–34). In the midst of their "great contest in the face of suffering" (v. 32), they made radical stands for Christ and His people because they knew they "had better and lasting possessions."

What has God promised those who suffer? First, He promises that our hardship will result in righteousness and holiness. "Endure hardship as discipline; God is treating you as sons" (Hebrews 12:7a). "God disciplines us for our good, that we may share in his holiness. No discipline seems pleasant at the time, but painful. Later on, however, it produces a harvest of righteousness and peace for those who have been trained by it" (vv. 10b–11). Through our hardship, God promises to make us more like Himself.

Second, God promises to be with us in our trials. "Fear not, for I have redeemed you; I have summoned you by name; you are mine. When you pass through the waters, I will be with you; and when you pass through the rivers, they will not sweep over you. When you walk through the fire, you will not be burned; the flames will not set you ablaze. Do not be afraid, for I am with you" (Isaiah 43:1–2, 5a). God remains with us when we suffer for His Son. He does not abandon us in our time of need. He promises, and we may trust His promise.

Third, God promises deliverance. This was the apostle Paul's confidence when he considered his most severe afflictions. At one point he felt as though a death sentence had been written in his heart and despaired of living any longer. Then he remembered: "This happened that we might not rely on ourselves but on God, who raises the dead. He has delivered us from such a deadly peril, and he will deliver us. On him we have set our hope that he will continue to deliver us" (2 Corinthians 1:9–10). Elsewhere the apostle wrote, "God is faithful; he will not let you be tempted beyond what you can bear. But when you are tempted, he will also provide a way out so that you can stand up under it" (1 Corinthians 10:13). The Father limits our suffering and grants deliverance.

And to these promises of God's sanctification, presence, and deliverance, we may add all the promises of the gospel—forgiveness of sin, reconciliation and peace with God, eternal life, resurrection, grace, and hope. Suffering is the crucible where the promises of God are ground more deeply into our souls. As a result, we're made more like Him and we endure with joy.

. . . BY REMEMBERING YOUR REWARD

For many, the prospect of suffering for Christ seems like a thankless job. It's all drudgery and despair. But the New Testament makes staggering promises about a coming reward for those who suffer in Christ's name.

Jesus promised in Matthew 5:10, "Blessed are those who are persecuted because of righteousness, for theirs is the kingdom of heaven." He also told His followers to "rejoice and be glad, because great is your reward in heaven" when men mistreat you because of Him (v. 12). We are to remember that our mistreatment by men is accompanied by reward from God. Though the suffering of this life be great, it is not worthy to be compared to the glory to come. Our present sufferings are light and momentary in comparison (see

Romans 8:17–18; 1 Peter 4:13). Our reward will be to share in Christ's glory with Him when He comes. Remembering that helps us to experience joy in the midst of our pains.

WHY DISCUSS SUFFERING IN A BOOK ON EVANGELISM?

Can you think of anything that conjures the fear of suffering like personal evangelism? Fear may so immobilize us that evangelism simply becomes a synonym for suffering. We need to address this neglected topic so we might experience the liberating power of the Spirit and the Scripture. More specifically, there are five reasons to address suffering and evangelism, especially as we present the gospel to Muslim friends.

> EXPECT SUFFERING *so that you can "rejoice that you participate in the sufferings of Christ" (v. 12).*

First, knowing the Bible's teaching on suffering can prepare us to rejoice when it comes rather than be surprised. Some Christians feel fear thinking of suffering. Others are surprised God would let them suffer. They should not be, says Peter (1 Peter 4:12). But imagine . . . we can rejoice at suffering.

Many times Christians lose heart and joy because their afflictions surprise them. They stumble spiritually because they were caught unawares by their trials. They even conclude wrongly that their struggles are evidence that God is displeased with them or that they are out of God's will. This is why Peter says to expect suffering so that we can "rejoice that you participate in the sufferings of Christ" (1 Peter 4:13), and James says "consider it pure joy" when we fall into trials of various kinds (James 1:2).

If we expect the trials as evidence of our living faithful Christian lives, we can rejoice that the suffering is a badge of our sincere faith.

Second, knowing the Bible's teaching on suffering can help us to shun the convenience and carnal pleasure that otherwise could dominate our lives. Though we wish to live at peace with all men, it's not peace at all costs. We are not willing to gain peace at the cost of righteousness, integrity, justice, and loyalty to Christ. Because the Lord conforms us to Himself (Romans 8:28–29; 1 Corinthians 15:49), we may expect that He will not leave us in the mold of this world (see Romans 12:1–2; 1 John 2:15–17). Our suffering is one way He weans us from the world and makes us fit for heaven. Through suffering God conquers our fleshly desires and our earth-bound affections. It's one way our loving Father teaches us to live for the right things.

Third, by knowing the Bible's teaching on suffering, we need not be afraid of Muslims when we share the gospel. Repeatedly Jesus instructs His disciples in Matthew 10 to not be afraid (vv. 26, 28, and 31). If we let fear drive us, we will wish to avoid all hardship, and we will fail to tell others the good news of God's love through Christ. In most of my failures as an evangelist—and there are many—somewhere in my heart fear found a home. I can think of many moments that seemed just right for a word of gospel hope where I withered in fears of various sorts. Even now I kick myself. But at the time, the fear of man, of rejection, of confrontation, of losing face, or some other mild suffering kept me from sharing the words of life.

Have you felt that way? If so, realize that with a good and right theology of suffering you can witness with less fear. Fear of suffering sidelines us in this great cosmic contest in which Christ is already victorious.

Fourth, knowing the Bible's teaching on suffering will help us prepare Muslim converts to endure suffering. Most Muslims awakened to faith in Christ will probably face immediate persecution. That's the way it was in the New Testament world, and that's the way it is in most of the Muslim world. So we would be negligent as makers of disciples if we left off this most fundamental lesson: Everyone who

> **A RIGHT THEOLOGY**
> *of suffering will bring more intimate fellowship with Christ.*

wishes "to live a godly life in Christ Jesus will be persecuted" (2 Timothy 3:12).

Our task is to teach Muslim-background converts all the things that Christ has commanded (Matthew 28:19–20), which includes His teachings about how to endure suffering with joy and hope. If we don't know this, and if we can't communicate that the riches of Christ far surpass the losses (Philippians 3:7–11), we will not serve people well in their new lives as Christians. We need a solid theology of suffering in order to carry on the important work of establishing disciples.

Fifth, having a right theology of suffering will bring more intimate fellowship with Christ. If we think that suffering is to be avoided at all costs, we will miss the unique communion with Jesus that only comes by sharing in His afflictions. The New Testament astounds us when it declares that because of our union with Christ we share in His life—both the sufferings and the comforts. "For just as the sufferings of Christ flow over into our lives, so also through Christ our comfort overflows" (2 Corinthians 1:5). The apostle Paul was driven in his desire to know Christ, so he joyfully sought to share in "the power of his resurrection and the fellowship of sharing in his sufferings" so that he might become "like him in his death" (Philippians 3:10).

A GREATER TREASURE

A good evangelist to the Muslim next door or at work—or to any person hostile or misinformed about Jesus—can expect challenge and suffering. Be careful not to shun suffering for the name of Christ. Look to the rewards He promises, including closer fellowship with the Savior, and continue on.

Remember the rich young man who asked Jesus, "What good thing must I do to gain eternal life?" Jesus replied, "Go, sell your possessions and give to the poor, and you will have treasure in heaven. Then come, follow me" (Matthew 19:21). We're told that this young man went away sad because he had great wealth. In other words, he didn't want to suffer loss in this world for life in the next.

He was a foolish man. Christ is a greater treasure than all the world can offer. It's the promise of life with Christ now and for eternity that makes suffering a small thing. Remember this truth as you present the gospel to Muslims. Remind Muslim friends that the cost of conversion and a commitment to Christ are worth it. For those who follow Christ have a new life and an eternal hope. And one day, when we see Him, "we shall be like him" (1 John 3:2) and we shall be satisfied (Psalm 17:15).

Things *to* Remember

1. When you experience suffering in the cause of Christ, keep your eyes on Jesus, remember God's promises, and look forward to your reward. "Great is your reward in heaven," Jesus says (Matthew 5:12).

2. Suffering is not unusual for people who live for Christ. We may expect it. So preparing for it and teaching others to endure it is a necessary part of what it means to make disciples. Muslim converts in particular will need this lesson modeled and taught well.

The Good News
for African-American Muslims

Islam is a religion with a fair amount of diversity. Arab Muslims differ from those practitioners of a syncrenistic folk Islam in Indonesia, who differ from African-American Muslims.

So an important question to ask when sharing the Good News with Muslims in America is: What kind of Muslim am I speaking with? There are a few key differences between traditional, or orthodox, Arab Muslims and African-American Muslims. Significantly, African-American Muslims are the fastest growing community of Muslims in the United States. If we're going to reach these neighbors and friends, it'll be helpful to know something about their unique perspective.

As a new convert to Islam, I was fascinated with the strength I saw in African-American Muslim men. They lived clean lives, spoke highly of family and community, and took up the cause of justice on behalf of the poor and oppressed. I'd never met African-American men like these.

HANGING OUT WITH SALEEM

Saleem was one such brother. He was devoted to his wife and tender toward her. He had a beautiful family—three playful boys and two doting daughters. He worked hard at a full-time job and accepted the occasional part-time opportunity so that his wife could remain home with the children. Whenever there was a need in the community, Saleem was sure to help. We routinely joked with him about the "strays" he would bring home, young men who seemed always to have some odd habits or out-of-the-way need. Saleem was a good man.

And I enjoyed my years of hanging out with him. They were long nights of fiery conversations about everything from history to politics and current events, from male-female relationships to theology. It's from Saleem and a handful of other Muslim friends that I learned the dominant narrative among African-American Muslims. The narrative can be summed up in four objections to Christianity.

HISTORY AND IDENTITY

African Muslims first reached the Americas during the Transatlantic slave trade. Islam had made inroads into West Africa well before the slave trade reached its peak. Many of the enslaved Africans were faithful practitioners.

This historical footnote has an interesting effect on

many of today's African-American Muslims. It adds a note of pride. Many African-Americans will think of Islam as more indigenous to African peoples, culture, and history than Christianity. They believe that to be a Muslim is in some way to be more "authentically black."

The radical teachings of the Nation of Islam and Malcolm X in America have much to do with this perspective. Malcolm and the Nation vilified Christianity as "the white man's religion," with its "blond-haired, blue-eyed Jesus."

Make sure that our friends do not think we're asking them to "sell out" their own history and culture. After all, Christianity has roots in Africa far more ancient than either the slave trade or Islam.

MAKE SURE THAT *our friends do not think we're asking them to "sell out" their own history and culture. After all, Christianity has roots in Africa far more ancient than either the slave trade or Islam.*

When we're sharing the gospel with African-American Muslims, we're not just having a religious conversation. We're often having a discussion about racial identity. So, we need to be careful to listen well. And where we can, we need to make sure that our friends do not think we're attacking who they are or asking them to "sell out" their own history and culture. After all, Christianity has roots in Africa far more ancient than either the slave trade or Islam.

POLITICS

African-American Islam, whether the Nation of Islam or more orthodox expressions like W. Deen Muhammad's American Muslim Movement, tends to blend closely with a Black Nationalist political philosophy.[1] For many African-Americans, Islam represents a certain reactionary posture toward Western society, history, and values. As a faith, Islam strengthens the political and activist resolve for greater autonomy, power and self-determination in the face of oppression and disenfranchisement.

This isn't completely unique to African-American Muslims. Remember the nurse Jamal in chapter 7? He spent twenty minutes telling me his view of Arab and American relations before he turned to spiritual issues. I've had that experience dozens of times. But with African-American Muslims, many white Christians may find themselves intimidated and ill-equipped for the commingling of Islam with racial identity and political philosophy. They may be tempted to avoid speaking of Jesus altogether for fear of heated debate.

THE BLACK CHURCH

Many African Americans will also be critical of the historic African-American church. For them, the church has long ceased being a prophetic voice for justice and equality. Many see the church as an organization too accommodating to white privilege and power, and therefore responsible for slowing African-American progress.

The church's preaching of a white Savior diminishes the

self-worth and self-reliance of African-American people. Muslims contend that if whites may make God in their image, then blacks certainly need to worship and serve a Black God. To the extent the historic black church fails on this score, African-American Muslims tend to disregard its claims and efforts. They see Christianity as an enslaving, colonizing force used by both white oppressors of African Americans and their black surrogates.

TRUE MANHOOD AND WOMANHOOD

African-American Muslims generally take family seriously. They tend to have large families organized in traditional gender roles of male leadership and female submission. For African-Americans, Islam can be seen as the only force that restores healthy family life, including strong male providers and virtuous wives and mothers.

The devastation of black family life is sometimes attributed to what is seen as an emasculating Christian influence. Christian men are viewed as weak. African-American Muslims object to women-dominated churches and homes. So much of the success of Islam in African-American communities comes from the Muslim community's ability to rehabilitate and strengthen African-American men and its concern for the protection of African-American family.

SOME SUGGESTIONS

A short, powerful narrative emerges from these objections. Islam gets tied to the survival of the African-American community, while Christianity is saddled with many of the ills of the black community. Liberation requires abandonment of the Christian faith. Empowerment means adoption of Islam as a lifestyle, political philosophy, and identity that repairs the injustices of centuries of mistreatment.

Well, how do we reach our African-American Muslim friends if so many obstacles stand in the way? In truth, African-American Muslims aren't any more difficult to reach than Arab Muslims, or your local atheist, or your Hindu neighbor. The objections simply grow out of a history of racial interactions that leave some feeling vulnerable. But the same gospel that saved us is the gospel that saves African-American Muslims, of which I was one.

Here are a few things to keep in mind as you speak with African-American Muslims about Jesus.

Use the church experiences most African-Americans will have. Even if your African-American Muslim friend is hostile to the black church, chances are he or she has spent some time in the black church. Moreover, it's highly likely that some significant family member—mother or grandmother—continues to be a faithful part of a local congregation. There will be some fond memories and some respect for the faith of their family members, however misguided they believe that faith to be.

A helpful place to begin might be with the good memories they have of the church or with the things they respect about their loved ones' faith. Particularly if you're attempting to share the gospel across ethnic lines, from outside the African-American experience, asking about positive assessments of the African-American community—including the church—can help lead toward fruitful spiritual conversations. Most African-American Muslims will have at least some Christian categories and church exposure useful for working toward the cross of Christ.

Concede issues wherever possible. When an African-American Muslim begins to enumerate the historical injustices African Americans have faced, or to espouse political opinions you do not share, pray and avoid debating with them. Wherever possible, concede points that are plausible. Who can argue against the brutality of chattel slavery? Who can legitimately defend Jim Crow segregation? And can we be confident that every instance of racism has been stamped out of society? If we're humble and honest, we must admit that tragic things have happened and sometimes still do. I would never defend the Crusades when attempting to talk with Muslims about Jesus. Likewise, offering a defense of slavery with African Americans simply won't be useful. It will distract from the main issue—the cross of Christ. So, wherever you can, concede such issues. And more than that, where possible condemn racism and mistreatment of others. Press home the need for individuals to trust in Christ to save them from their sins.

Finally, *demonstrate the alternative of a loving personal community.* For all of its rhetoric about a universal brotherhood and community, in my opinion Islam fails to live up to its claim. In the African-American context, "the community" tends to mean all African Americans abstractly. What this often means is that many African Americans—Muslims included—actually live in pockets of vast alienation. "Community" means holding to the same political philosophy and identity politics. It often fails to mean close, loving, personal relationships.

But the Christian church, by definition, includes spiritual oneness with Christ and with each other Christian. Christian churches can fail to be places of genuine community. But where such communities do exist, they provide a powerful counter-narrative to that held by most African-American Muslims. That counter-narrative reveals how hollow a philosophical and political "community" can be. There's nothing like tangible love to compel people to consider the truth about Jesus (John 13:34–35). And where those communities practice biblical teaching on family and gender roles, they take away one attractive feature of African-American Islam.

Things *to* Remember

1. Most African-American Muslims will have had some exposure to Christianity and Christian ideas. Remember to use these points of contact as starting points for clarifying and explaining the gospel.

2. Be patient in discussions with African-American Muslims. Realize that many conversations about religion are also tied together with important identity issues. Avoid critical comments about ethnic identity or politics and focus more directly on clarifying the gospel, repentance and faith.

Afterword

Just over a decade ago, I was an enemy of the cross. I opposed the gospel of my Lord and His people. I'm not sure I could have been harder in my entire outlook.

And now, God has saved me. And not only has He saved me, but He has given me the great privilege of preaching His gospel and shepherding His people. I can't imagine a bigger reversal in so short a time! I look back over the years that I've been a Christian and wonder at the riches of God's grace.

From time to time, the Lord grants me the privilege of participating in dialogue and conversation with Muslims. Through those encounters, He gives me small glimpses into His inexhaustible wisdom. While one part of me laments the days spent lost in Islam, another part rejoices that God had an amazing purpose in allowing me to spend prodigal years as a Muslim in order to redeem that experience as a Christian evangelist and pastor. I cry out with another former enemy of the cross, the apostle Paul, "Oh, the depth of the riches of the wisdom and knowledge of God! How unsearchable his judgments, and his paths beyond tracing out!" (Romans 11:33).

And with the apostle I marvel at God's kindness: "Even though I was once a blasphemer and a persecutor and a violent man, I was shown mercy because I acted in ignorance and unbelief. The grace of our Lord was poured out on me abundantly, along with the faith and love that are in Christ Jesus" (1 Timothy 1:13–14).

When it comes to Muslim evangelism, the greatest myth is that Muslims do not convert. I'm here to tell you that they do. But don't take my word for it. Take God's Word: "The gospel . . . is the power of God for the salvation of everyone who believes: first for the Jew, then for the Gentile" (Romans 1:16)—including the Muslim Gentile.

Don't stop with my story. Go out and play your part in God's bigger story of bringing people from every nation to a saving knowledge of His Son and into eternal life!

I believe in the power of God in the gospel. Like you, my Christian reader, I have tasted that power and been born again. And I believe that this same gospel is the power of God to win our Muslim neighbors, friends, and coworkers to Christ. We know enough in the gospel itself to help Muslim people find eternal life through the Son of God. Let us joyfully tell the good news!

Notes

Chapter 1: God by Any Other Name?

1. From time to time, avoiding conversations about Christian views of the Quran may prove difficult. If you need to give an informed response, helpful and readable information is available in Norman L. Geisler and Abdul Saleeb, *Answering Islam* (Grand Rapids: Baker, 2002) and Colin Chapman, *Cross and Crescent* (Downers Grove, Ill.: InterVarsity, 2003).

Chapter 2: Man's Sin: Resting Lightly on the Muslim Conscience

1. Chawkat Moucarry, *The Prophet and the Messiah: An Arab Christian's Perspective on Islam and Christianity* (Downers Grove, Ill.: InterVarsity, 2001), 99.

2. J. Budziszewski, *The Revenge of Conscience* (Dallas: Spence Publishing, 2004).

3. John Piper, *Brothers, We Are Not Professionals:* (Nashville: Broadman and Holman, 2002), 114–15.

4. Ibid., 115.

5. "Nabil" is a fictional name used to protect a Muslim convert. He is the subject of a biography written by David Zeidan, *The Fifth Pillar* (Carlisle, UK: Piquant, 2000), 78.

6. Zeidan, *The Fifth Pillar*, 78.

Chapter 3: Jesus Christ: Fully God and Fully Man

1. A number of helpful books have been written in recent years. Those interested in further study on this topic might be interested in two books by Randy Newman: *Questioning Evangelism: Engaging People's Hearts the Way Jesus Did* (Grand Rapids: Kregel, 2004) and *Corner Conversations: Engaging Dialogues about God and Life* (Grand Rapids: Kregel, 2006). Mack Stiles's *Speaking of Jesus: How to Tell Your Friends the Best News They Will Ever Hear* (Downers Grove, Ill.: InterVarsity, 1995) is well worth the reading time. As is Mark Dever's *The Gospel and Personal Evangelism* (Wheaton: Crossway, 2007).

2. C. S. Lewis, *Mere Christianity*, rev. ed. (New York: Collier, 1952), 55–56.

Chapter 4: Jesus Christ: the Lamb Slain—and Resurrected!

1. Khaled Hosseini, *The Kite Runner* (New York: Riverhead, 2003), 76–77.

2. This is the view offered, for example, by Phil Parshall, *Muslim Evangelism* (Waynesboro, Ga.: Gabriel Publishing, 2003), 159–61.

3. Bruce K. Waltke with Cathi J. Fredricks, *Genesis* (Grand Rapids: Zondervan, 2001), 244–45.

4. J. Gresham Machen, *Christianity and Liberalism* (1923; repr., Grand Rapids: Eerdmans, 2009), 135–36.

Chapter 5: Response: There's Repentance and Faith . . .

1. Wayne Grudem, *Bible Doctrine* (Grand Rapids: Zondervan, 1999), 310.

2. C. John Miller, *Repentance and 21st Century Man* (Fort Washington, Pa.: CLC Publications, 1975), 26.

3. James Montgomery Boice, *The Gospel of John, Vol. 1: The Coming of the Light, John 1–4* (Grand Rapids: Baker, 1999), 224–25.

4. For a clear and useful discussion of these issues, see Chawkat Moucarry, *The Search for Forgiveness: Pardon and Punishment in Islam and Christianity* (Downers Grove, Ill.: InterVarsity, 2004); see chapter 9. For a brief overview of Islamic teaching on sin, see chapter 7 in *The Search for Forgiveness*, and chapter 2 of this book.

5. John Piper, *Finally Alive* (Minneapolis: Christian Focus and Desiring God Ministries, 2009), 28.

Chapter 7: Trust the Bible

1. Keep in mind, this book is not a book on apologetics. There are times and places where a more thorough defense of the Scriptures is warranted. But defending the Bible is not the same thing as proclaiming the gospel, doing the work of an evangelist. To share the gospel, all we need is sufficient dependence on the reliability of the Scriptures, which we simply need assert as our Muslim friends assert the reliability of the Quran.

2. For a good brief treatment of this issue, see Moucarry, *The Prophet and the Messiah*, 44–79.

3. See, for example, Sura 2:285; 3:93–94; 4:163–165; 5:46–48; 6:91–92; 17:55; and 21:103.

Chapter 8: Be Hospitable

1. Shirin Taber, *Muslims Next Door: Uncovering Myths and Creating Friendships* (Grand Rapids: Zondervan, 2004), 114.

2. Ibid., 96.

Chapter 9: Use Your Local Church

1. Paul Laurence Dunbar, *The Collected Poetry of Paul Laurence Dunbar*, ed. Joanne M. Braxton (1913; repr., Charlottesville: Univ. Press of Virginia, 1993).

2. Joshua Harris, *Stop Dating the Church* (Sisters, Oreg.: Multnomah, 2004), 47–48.

3. Charles Bridges, *The Christian Ministry* (Edinburgh: Banner of Truth Trust, 2005), 1.

Chapter 10: Suffer for the Name

1. In saying this, I don't mean to suggest that Christians have no right to defend themselves or that governments have no right to protect themselves. Romans 13 establishes the right of governments to exercise the sword. And Jesus' instruction to disciples to avoid coming persecution (Matthew 10:23, for example) makes it clear that Christians are not seeking suffering. Christians are to escape suffering where possible and where such escape does not amount to denying their Lord. However, retaliatory violence motivated by hateful aggression is condemned by Scripture.

2. Ajith Fernando, *The Call to Joy and Pain* (Wheaton: Crossway, 2007), 79.

3. Ibid., 80.

Chapter 11: The Good News for African-American Muslims

1. African-American Islam is quite diverse. The earliest organizational expressions of Islam were Noble Drew Ali's Moorish Science Temple, founded in 1913. The Nation of Islam, popularly known as "Black Muslims," began in the 1930s under the leadership of Farhud Muhammad, called by followers Master Fard or Farhud. Elijah Muhammad, an early student of Farhud Muhammad, took over the Nation of Islam's leadership after the curious disappearance of Farhud Muhammad. Elijah Muhammad led the organization until his death in 1975. Some years before his death, the Nation of Islam experienced organizational troubles as its most famous adherent, Malcolm X, led a group of Muslims out of the Nation of Islam to form a more orthodox organization. Malcolm's movement was short lived. But soon Elijah Muhammad's son, W. Deen Muhammad, followed Malcolm's steps and founded what is known today as the American Society of Muslims, a Sunni Muslim group of African-Americans. Louis Farrahkan succeeded Elijah Muhammad as the leader of the Nation of Islam. Various other groups of African-American Muslims have sprouted across the U.S., including the Ansaru Allah or Nubian Islamic Hebrews and the Five Percent Nation of Islam.

For further reading, see, Clifton Marsh, *From Black Muslims to Muslims: The Transition from Separatism to Islam* (Meteushen, N.J.: Scarecrow Press, 1984); and Elijah Muhammad, *Message to the Black Man in America* (Chicago: Muhammad Mosque of Islam No. 2, 1965).